CW01022802

THE INWARD ROAD
and the way back

THE INWARD ROAD
and the way back

Texts and Reflections
on
Religious Experience

Dorothee Sölle

translated by
David L. Scheidt

Wipf and Stock Publishers
EUGENE, OREGON

This book is a translation of *Die Hinreise: Zur religiösen Erfahrung, Texte und Überlegungen,* copyright © 1975 by Kreuz Verlag in Stuttgart, Germany.

Biblical quotations from the Revised Standard Version of the Bible, copyright 1946, 1952, © 1971, 1973 by the Division of Christian Education of the National Council of the Churches of Christ in the U.S.A., are used by permission.

Wipf and Stock Publishers
199 W 8th Ave, Suite 3
Eugene, OR 97401

The Inward Road and the Way Back
By Sölle, Dorothee
Copyright© by Soelle, Dorothee
ISBN 13: 978-1-59244-192-1
Publication date 3/15/2003
Previously published by Fortress Press,

Contents

PART ONE

INTRODUCTION

1

Death by Bread Alone

"Man does not live by bread alone."[1] In fact, bread alone kills us. To live by bread alone is to die a slow and dreadful death in which all human relationships are mutilated and strangled. Of course, such a death by bread alone does not mean that we cease to exist. Our bodies still function. We still go about the chores and routines of life; we accomplish things; we breathe; we produce and consume and excrete; we come, go, and speak. Yet we do not really live. In Samuel Beckett's play *Happy Days* there is a character by the name of Winnie, a woman of about fifty. In the first act Winnie is buried in sand up to her waist; nonetheless she chatters away, brushes her teeth, rummages about in her handbag, and feels sorry for her husband. In the second act she is buried up to her chin and can no longer move her head. All relationships are severed, but that stream of idle chatter, in which she takes herself so seriously, flows on and on. That is a kind of death; that is what hell is like, being buried in sand, unable to change things and yet without pain, content to while away the time. "Abandon hope all ye who enter here"; this is the living death by bread alone.

Death by bread alone means being alone and then wanting to be left alone; being friendless, yet distrusting and despising

3

others; forgetting others and then being forgotten; living only for ourselves and then feeling unneeded; being unconcerned about others and wanting no one to be concerned about us; neither laughing nor being laughed at; neither crying for another nor being cried for by another. How horrible is this death by bread alone.

I have a neighbor, an elderly, childless man whose wife died not long ago. One day he called me over to show me some damage, the scratches some children had made on his property with their bicycles. "Just look at what they have done," he said, "this house is all we have." Man dies by bread alone. My neighbor had worked for what he had. He lived in that house, kept it in repair, took care of it. "This house is all we have," he had said. Suddenly it dawned on me that this man was dead. He had died from no longer having any kind of relationship with another human being.

This is what the Bible means when it speaks of death. Death is what takes place within us when we look upon others not as gift, blessing, or stimulus but as threat, danger, competition. It is the death that comes to all who try to live by bread alone. This is the death that the Bible fears and gives us good reason to fear. It is not the final departure we usually think of when we speak of death; it is that purposeless, empty existence devoid of genuine human relationships and filled with anxiety, silence, and loneliness.

"I am reckoned among those who go down to the Pit," the psalmist cries.[2] He is speaking here of himself as one who is already dead, who has been laid away in the grave and now dwells in darkness, friendless and in misery.

> I am a man who has no strength,
> like one forsaken among the dead,
>   like the slain that lie in the grave,
> like those whom thou dost remember no more,
>   for they are cut off from thy hand.

Thou hast put me in the depths of the Pit,
in the regions dark and deep.
Thy wrath lies heavy upon me,
and thou dost overwhelm me with all thy waves.
Thou hast caused my companions to shun me;
thou hast made me a thing of horror to them.
I am shut in so that I cannot escape;
my eye grows dim through sorrow.[3]

Grief isolates us. It kills us by destroying the relationships that are the heartthrob of life. We experience the same grief, depression, and defeat that the psalmist experienced; it is death by bread alone.

The death of which the Bible speaks lays hold of us in the very midst of life. It is the boredom and emptiness of going through the motions of living while being totally drained of all humanity and reduced to the level of an old work horse.

The parable of the prodigal son is an example of the death the Bible talks about.[4] The prodigal son went off to a far country with high hopes, but he ended up tending another man's swine. He worked for starvation wages, for bread alone. In short, he lived by bread alone. This is why his father spoke of him as being dead. The prodigal son had no human ties. There was no one with whom he could speak. He was something to be used. There among the swine he simply vegetated away without any hope that things would change for him. According to the Bible, this kind of existence cannot be called living. It is simply vegetating, going through the motions of living. To be sure, the prodigal son went through the motions, but he certainly was not living. Existing there among the swine was death in the midst of life. This is how the prodigal son's father saw it. Jesus saw it that way too. We have to make the same distinction between existing and living. "*Survivre n'est pas vivre,*" "to survive does not mean one is living." (University students wrote this on the walls of Paris in May 1968.) Struggling along, surviving, trying to make ends meet—that certainly is not living. On the contrary, that is the very death that threatens to swallow us up.

"In the midst of life we are in death."[5] And this does not mean death by cancer or accident; after all, we do not need to be made aware of our mortality—that is a heathen, aesthetic matter. What it means is the death that surrounds us on every side in the very midst of life: the death of alienation, loneliness. For the most part we do not find it difficult to pass from one stage of life to another. What is really difficult, if not utterly impossible, is attaining to a stage or condition of life in which such words as "leavetaking" and "grief" still have any meaning. We are so alienated from other people that we experience neither the bitterness nor the sweetness of grief. This is the hell that swallows us up in the very midst of life as we go about the motions and routines of life. Death is the wages of sin, the consequence of inauthentic life. It means to be so estranged from others that we can trust no one. Death is a life that is nothing but surviving.

Because we live for bread alone, we die by bread alone. Death by bread alone is not a natural death. It is a violent death, one that is imposed upon us by the structures of violence that rule this world. We willingly accept this state of affairs. And when the truth is told, we even prefer being dead to taking the kind of risks involved with being alive. And there are risks! The person who is really alive, who isn't buried in sand while chattering away, who still feels and is touched and moved by what goes on in the world, by what happens to others, is one who runs the risk of going mad in a society that lives for bread alone and subordinates all other concerns to that of profit.

I speak here for the growing number of people in mental institutions and psychiatrists' offices—the people we call emotionally and mentally disturbed—because they are the ones who are struggling against the death that surrounds us on every side. These people are the vicarious substitutes for those of us who think of ourselves as "healthy" because we go on playing the game. They represent a kind of life—to put it more correctly, a crying out for life—in a world that is ruled by violent death. Like Abel, they are put out of the way. The first death of which the Bible tells us is the murder of Abel by his brother Cain.⁶ That murder was an act of personal violence. But in our world this violence has become quite impersonal, indeed, even institutionalized, and it rides roughshod over any and all. It imposes itself on life; it likes to tidy life up and put things in order. It ruins life.

Bertolt Brecht puts it this way: "There are many ways to kill. We can thrust a knife into someone's belly, or let him starve to death. We can withhold medication or treatment of an illness, or we can force someone to live in substandard housing. We can simply work someone to death, or drive him to suicide, or send him off to war. Very little of this is forbidden in our country."⁷

There is no end to the ways in which we can destroy life. We can rob children of their childhood simply by forbidding them to move about and make noise. Our very systems of education can destroy them by killing the joy of learning and the curiosity that makes them want to learn. There are many ways to kill! We can construct housing developments and plan cities in such a way that even though people live in close physical proximity to each other they have the fewest possible relationships with each other. For example, we can put two people of different race or language side by side at a place of employment and thereby guarantee that no relationship or communication of more than a superficial nature can develop and that production will not be impeded.

There are many ways to kill! The impersonal structure of bureaucracy and red tape can intimidate and harass a person to the point that he will take his life. Indeed, it is possible to structure human relationships and contacts within the context of employment in such a way that while people can function efficiently and with a minimum of personal friction, they are virtually strangers to each other.

Unlike the prodigal son, people today do not purposely seek out strange and alien places where, devoid of ties and relationships, they tend the swine of others. It is the structures of violence that force them to do it. The alienation that the Bible calls death is built into life at the most important point—at our work. Being dead is something that is learned; we are educated to be dead. It is in the area of work that life has been fragmented into bits and pieces that we think we can control and manage. But the fragments become meaningless and the whole process is an accommodation to death. This kind of death is not part of our human nature. It is something that we have been taught since childhood. This is the death of which the Bible speaks.

If profit is the one thing to which all else in this life is subordinated, then everything else is of no significance. We can take or leave everything else, be for it or against it. One person can be interested in the homeless; another in racing cars. One person may like animals; another, children. One person may prefer the snow-crested mountains; another the seashore. You see, life is a gigantic supermarket in which we can have everything we want. But there is no longer any reason we should want one thing rather than the other.

If life is just a matter of buying and selling, then relationships too become just so many purchasable commodities. Today many perceive the world as just such a supermarket. Absent-mindedly, yet at the same time absorbed in what we are doing, we push our shopping carts up one aisle and down the other while death and alienation have the run of the place. It is said that people watch television on the average of four and a half hours each day. If that is true, then how can any meaningful relationships develop out of that kind of environment? The world is nothing but a supermarket and a factory concerned for bread alone, living for bread alone. Death is the order of the day, and each day we die that dreadful death by bread alone.

This is the death of which the Bible speaks. The Bible calls it the "wages of sin,"[8] the "last enemy."[9] It was against just this kind of death that Jesus organized resistance. The stories that tell of the raising of Lazarus[10] and Jairus's daughter[11] from the dead deal with the struggle against death by bread alone and encourage us not to accept death but to have faith. To have faith means to take a stand for life. The conquest of death is first announced not in Jesus' resurrection but in the stories connected with his life. Death reigns where violence and alienation run rampant. The more we live without human relationships, the more we accept and tolerate death. We don't care about bloodshed in Africa, even though the weapons that cause it come from our factories. We don't care about the staggering infant mortality rate among dark-skinned peoples in distant lands, even though there is a relationship between that mortality rate in the exploited lands and increased profits.

We live in alienation, and our concern is to avoid pain and do whatever is necessary to put food on the table and make ends meet. Because we live by bread alone, we tolerate violence and perpetuate its structures. We give our allegiance to whatever seems to support this state of affairs. That's how we arrange our lives. We love anything that makes us unfeeling. We serve whatever regiments us and reduces us to just another number in the computer. Psychoanalyst Erich Fromm calls this kind of love necrophilia, an obsession with what is dead, categorized, regulated, controlled, stripped of spontaneity and desire.[12]

But the political and bureaucratic spheres of life are not the only ones in which this necrophilia prevails. Even our churches are filled with it, for the churches are quite comfortable with whatever they can organize, record, formulate dogmatically, accommodate within institutional structures. The church is enamored of the kind of Christ which, 450 years ago, Thomas Müntzer called the "honeysweet Christ," that is, a Christ who "is acceptable to our murderous nature." This "honeysweet Christ" guarantees us a comfortable existence and throws eternal life into the bargain. This Christ doesn't disturb or threaten our armaments industry and he even gives some semblance of meaning to our comfortable daily routine. We necrophiliacs worship God as a being whose purpose is to preserve, not create; to govern, not change; to protect, not liberate. We think of God as some kind of nonpartisan being which is like an unfeeling computer that has been crammed full of varied information about people. But the God of whom the Bible speaks is not nonpartisan. He is highly partisan. He has taken sides with life against death. He despises death and fights against it wherever it shows itself, against death by napalm, starvation, by bread alone, by whatever stifles and strangles life.

To believe in God means to take sides with life and to end our alliance with death. It means to stop killing and wanting to kill, and to do battle with apathy which is so akin to killing. It means an end to the fear of dying and to its counterpart, the fear of failure. To take sides with life means to stop looking for some neutral ground between murderers and their victims and to cease looking upon the world as a supermarket in which we can buy anything we want so long as the price is right and the system is preserved.

Taking sides with life is not an easy or simple thing. It involves a never-ending process of change whereby we constantly renounce the self that is dead and enamored of death and instead become free to love life. To take sides with life and experience how we can transcend ourselves is a process that has many names and faces. Religion is one of those names. Religion can mean the radical and wholehearted attempt to take sides with life. This book has no intention of discussing religion as a concept, in abstract terms, nor is it yet another attempt to define religion. Rather, the intention of this book is to describe and communicate religious experiences. Our theme is the passing from death—our normal state—into life, and religion is seen as a basic means by which this passing is effected. What is the connection between religious experience and the achievement of personal identity? To what extent does religion help us truly to live?

What I have to say is said from a particular point of view. I am a Christian. When I seek help against that ever-present death by bread alone I turn instinctively to Jesus Christ, learning from him how to fight and conquer death. I do not claim, however, that this way is the only way to do so. I know many Jewish, humanist, socialist individuals and groups who, with the help of other guides and patrons and saints, fight the same battle and have similar experiences. As far as I am concerned it is not important or necessary that we all embrace the same faith, perhaps some common faith of humanity. What is important is that people be able to communicate and share their religious experiences.

Turning to religion must not mean turning away from each other but rather turning to each other. When I try to say what Christ means to me, threatened as I am by the strangling death that is all around us, I am trying to speak about the steps that can lead all of us out of the prevailing state of death. The recollection of Jesus derives its power not from "one-way" slogans and bumper-sticker theology but from what that recollection says about happiness, peace, love, and justice. It speaks of these things not as requirements or demands to be imposed upon humanity, but as things that can and do happen in the lives of each of us. One of the things the Jesus tradition says is that learning to love means also—indeed primarily—learning to die, and therein lies the offer of finding our identity.

Jesus took sides with life. He battled against death wherever he found it: the death of outcast lepers with whom none would speak, whom none would touch; the death of the publicans whom society held in utter contempt; the physical death of those who had not yet begun to live. Here note must be made of something without which Jesus' relationship to death cannot be understood. Neither Jesus nor those who, like him, battle against violent death looked upon physical death as the worst thing that can happen to us. They feared a life that is ruled and controlled by death more than they feared death itself. As Jesus saw it, it is worse to live a life that is strangled and suffocated by the death that prevails in the midst of life than it is to die and be laid in the grave. For Jesus and others like him natural death is by no means the greatest enemy. Rather, our greatest enemy is the kind of creeping death, that living, breathing lifelessness we see written on the faces of so many in our day. It is this kind of death and dying by bread alone that calls for our most resolute and passionate resistance and battle.

But Jesus' attitude toward death and that of others like him is contrary to ours. We prefer to cling tenaciously to the "honeysweet Christ." We want no part of the Christ of vinegar and gall. We accept more or less as fate the kind of death that surrounds us in all its forms, the kind of death imposed by society's structures and forces: war and starvation; robotized, impersonal existence; the monotony and routine of going through the motions of living. But what we struggle against is natural death from sickness and age, regarding it as our bitterest foe. It is natural death that we fight and resist with every means at our disposal. Our attitude comes to light in the newspaper death notices: an eighty-year-old man dies "suddenly" and "unexpectedly." This kind of wording suggests an attitude that physical death is something foreign to us, something that should not touch us. Our preoccupation with sexual enlightenment—prolongation of sexual activity, contraception, and erotic devices—suggests our childish refusal to accept natural, physical death, and our steadfast refusal to acknowledge, expect, or discuss it. In homes for the aged conversation about physical death is taboo; the residents of these institutions just will not tolerate such conversation. Even doctors and nurses are averse to talking about natural death. They do not want to hear such talk because it reminds them of their own mortality. The reluctance to talk about death with someone who is dying, the refusal to face up to death's reality, is something that grows on us. Such inhibitions are signs of a life that has not been lived. The less a person has really lived, experienced, and accomplished intellectually, emotionally, and sexually, in other words the less a person has lived up to life's possibilities, the more difficult it is to die.

In a very real sense this fear of natural death stems from the feeling of the individual that life owes him something. The person who has spent his life in working to accumulate, possess, and enjoy things simply has to resist every thought of death and in effect even deny that there is such a thing as death. Such resistance and denial is a fear that is rarely expressed in so many words. It is, nonetheless, the fear that enslaves all who live by bread alone. The person who has not found himself, who does not know who or what he is, can accept natural death only when physical circumstances compel him to do so. It should be the goal of the Christian to accept the reality of natural death and to learn to die.

The desire for a future life and for some form of continued personal existence is most deeply rooted in the resistance to death of those who have not lived an authentic and genuine life. The only weapon against such death is that of love. Those who die without ever having plunged into the stream of love die a hopeless death. Death can be accepted only by those who know what it means to live. Only they can take sides with life against the death that comes by bread alone.

Learning to die means no longer to hate or be burdened with

fear. To learn to die means to be caught up in a great chorus that affirms life; that is what faith is. The more we learn to live in freedom from fear the more we learn to die in freedom from fear. The more we are united to that love with which we know ourselves to be at one, the more immortal we are. As Christians we know that death always lies behind us; it is love that lies ahead. The Bible tells us: "We know that we have passed out of death into life, because we love the brethren. He who does not love remains in death."[13] Being a Christian means that we have passed from death to life. We have gone beyond death. In the case of a Christian, the biological order of birth followed by death is reversed. The Christian dies first, then he is born. Passing from death to life, the individual Christian will not need such a crutch as the hope of reunion in heaven with loved ones. Nor will the Christian need the crutch of a hope for continued personal existence in a heavenly realm. Absolutely nothing—not even the knowledge of our transitory personal existence—can separate us from the love of God. Nothing can separate us from the unending life to which we, in faith, have consented, just as nothing can separate a drop from the stream of which that drop is a constituent part. What would the stream be without its drops? What would God be without us? Indeed, what would love itself be without those who participate in it, who live in and from and for love?

Because nothing can separate us from the love of God,[14] we can live and bear the thought that we will no longer exist. With all our might we can resist that death of which the Bible speaks —death by bread alone, the death that stuffs yet chokes us while the other two-thirds of the world starves. We will be like Jesus, who took sides with life and could still accept his own death. Our energies are not consumed by the contradictions with which fear confronts us, for we have become free. It is no longer a question whether everything ends with death. The only people who can ask such a question are those who are so imprisoned within themselves that they have isolated themselves from the great reality that touches and changes us.

The question whether everything ends with death is a godless one. What does "everything" mean? How can the Christian say that everything is over when we die, knowing that in and of himself he is not everything. Of course, everything is not over —it goes on. To be sure, *I* will not eat anymore, but bread will still be baked and eaten. *I* will not drink anymore, but the cup that cheers will continue to be drunk. Nor will *I* breathe anymore as a person of the twentieth century, but the air will still be there for others to breathe.

We have been speaking so far about two kinds of death. One is the senseless, meaningless death of the prodigal son among the swine. Jesus speaks of this kind of death in the past tense, for the father says of his son, ". . . your brother was dead, and is alive. . . ."[15] Jesus speaks about this death as something that has been transcended. Who of us cannot tell such a story about himself? Have we not seen with our own eyes people who have been raised from the dead? Death with all its crippling fears and limitations is behind them. The prodigal son was dead but is alive, for in that moment when father and son approached each other the realm of death and alienation was left behind.

Another death about which the Bible speaks is that of Moses. God had granted Moses just before his death a glimpse of the Promised Land from the height of Mount Nebo. According to Scripture, Moses' eyes were not dimmed nor was his strength diminished.[16] Though he beheld the Promised Land, he knew he would not set foot upon it. Moses did not need the hope of a personal resurrection, nor did he fear the lesser, physical death, for in the enslavement in Egypt he had recognized and fought against the greater death which robs us of true life, the death that comes by bread alone. Moses could, therefore, accept and consent to natural, physical death. This is the kind of death that I pray for myself and wish for all. It is easier to die when we have caught a glimpse of the "Promised Land."

2

The Fear of Religion

What does religion mean? What does it have to do with death by bread alone? What can religion do to fight against the ever-present death which surrounds and threatens all of us? This is the basic question to which this book addresses itself.

Let me begin by sharing with you a personal experience from my student days. Originally my studies were concentrated in the fields of classical philology and philosophy. It was not until my sixth semester that I changed over to theology and the scientific study of literature. One day I ran into an acquaintance of my parents and in the course of conversation I mentioned that I had changed my course of studies. Her reaction was, "Oh? I did not realize you were so religious." Her remark shocked me. For years the memory of that remark has haunted me. From then on I simply avoided this lady. And ever since, the remark that someone is deeply religious has struck me as both unfortunate and impossible. Being religious had absolutely nothing to do with what I wanted to accomplish by studying theology.

I was not a "religious" person. I had no "prayer life," no relationship to anything supernatural and none whatsoever to the church. I simply wanted to know "the truth." I had not found it in philosophy—at least not in ways tangible or practical enough to meet my needs. It was my conviction that my life should not be eaten up by working and consuming; it should have some kind of direction to follow. For those of us who were students in the years after World War II, doing something with our lives was extremely important; we took it for granted even though we were not certain what it meant. If I try to put into words what we felt in those days, I would have to put it this way:

> to be total—to live an unfragmented life
> to be whole—not to be destroyed
> to make things whole—not to ruin or wreck things
> to hunger for justice—not to tolerate injustice
> to live an authentic life—not to be apathetic
> to go to heaven—not to stay in hell

I suppose all that sounds quite naive, yet these wishes were somehow grounded in the assumption that a sound, total life is not something that will someday be up yonder, but something to be lived consciously here and now. So then, theology was the study of exactly what its name claims: the study of God.

I could not bear the thought that most people go about the business of living simply by going through the motions, eking out a living, constantly concerned with surviving. Although I could understand such an attitude in those years just after the war, I began to perceive in it a tremendous self-contempt—a living out the days and weeks and years without really living. I did not recognize at that time that this self-contempt is one of the psychic undergirdings of the capitalist system. I saw the contempt that people who had come back from the war thoroughly demoralized and torn to shreds had for themselves. It was as though they had thrown themselves on the refuse heap. Somehow I sensed that it is this kind of self-contempt that the Bible calls godlessness. But I did not realize what political and economic factors lay beneath this self-contempt. My questions were richer and fuller than the so-called religious questions about the existence of another world. In spite of my negative reaction to her, was not that lady of whom I spoke a bit earlier at least a little bit right? Was not that which I desired for all—being whole, sound, not just as happy as possible but supremely happy—precisely what religion seeks and promises to all?

The word "religion" connotes the idea of aversion, of turning away. We are afraid of having a religion, of being religious. Most especially, we are afraid of the kind of religion that is practiced and taught by the professionally religious—clergymen, teachers, et al. For many, religion is very much like a hobby; it is a matter of choice and taste, something to be taken or left as one may choose. One does not get very far with this kind of game. The fact of the matter is that in our irreligious world religion is looked upon as something absurd, and its pronouncements and explanations evoke reactions that range from astonishment to disgust.

We are afraid of religion. At the end of a student seminar on fear, the attempt was made to speak on a personal rather than on an academic level. Each of the seminar students was asked to tell how he or she had overcome fear. A young woman told of her problems with her mother. It seems that her mother simply would not accept the daughter's fiancé. As a result, the daughter became ill over the situation and went from one doctor to another. She went on to tell how she and her fiancé had prayed together about the matter, that over a lengthy period of time their praying led to a solution of the problem that had been affecting her physically. While this experience shocked the other participants in the seminar, it had a liberating effect upon them as well. Someone in that group of academic theologians had broken a taboo and shared a relevant, personal, and human experience, not in the language used by others but in religious language, just as others told how they had overcome fear through participation in music groups, reading their original poems to each other, "letting down their hair." "If it had not been for prayer," she said, "we would have gotten nowhere." But the rest of us were afraid to show any sign of religion.

What I have just related is unusual in that what the student spoke of was a departure from the usual irreligious frame of mind. At the same time it is subject to misunderstanding. The irreligious world always fits every religious expression into the context of organized religion, that is, the church. To be sure, even a socialist must accept the fact that he is identified with socialism as it is practiced by the unions. People, however, are far more critical when it comes to religion. Like it or not, a person who is religious is identified with an institution that sometimes is jokingly said to provide "insurance against too much religion." People frequently associate all manner of unpleasantness with this institution, much of it stemming from forced attendance at services or at religious instruction. This was the only contact many ever had with religion. Unfortunately, we have to admit that many of these negative feelings are not unfounded. To have or wish for or show any sign of religion or of being religious is looked upon as being unenlightened, as holding prescientific if not outright superstitious views. Now, if scientific knowledge is the key by which we relate to the world about us, then everything apart from such knowledge takes on the appearance of being irrational.

The crisis confronts other than Christian expressions of religion as well. The critique of religion—which is an obvious factor in our spiritual condition—does not center primarily on the content of Christianity. The critique is rather a methodological critique directed at prescientific attempts to solve man's problems in a religious way. Consciously or not, we think of human history along the lines of the nineteenth-century idea of progress. This progress is depicted in three stages: magic, religion, science. Frazer put it this way:

> Ultimately the more advanced thinkers realized that magic did not accomplish what it was supposed to accomplish, and, because they still were not in the position of dealing with their problems with empirical tools or of meeting the crisis with a better philosophy, these thinkers came upon other illusions. They concluded that there are spiritual beings which could help them. In the course of time advanced minds saw that the business of spirits was a fraud. It was this insight which can be regarded as the dawning of experimental science.[1]

This observation by one of the outstanding experts in the field of religious studies sets forth the usual method of dealing with religion: questioning and analyzing. Religion is looked upon as the childhood stage of mankind. Religion has no function in an adult society that is in the process of maturing and emancipating itself from the remnants of its childhood. It does not require the slightest mental exertion to free oneself of religion; the critique of religion has asserted itself everywhere and has exerted a strong influence on the intellectual climate of our time. Against the background of widespread irreligiosity, religion represents a departure from the general run of things and a source of anxiety.

We are afraid of religion and of the community that goes hand in hand with it. It is difficult to control. We are afraid of the emotions that religion helps to articulate. We do not object to emotions so long as they are private and restrained. Nor do we object to a group dynamic that is totally wrapped up in itself. But the kind of religious emotions that are expressed in ways critical of the world are regarded as dangerous. For us such emotions are as much taboo as was conversation about sexual matters to our grandparents. To pray, to experience common aspirations, to share with one another our fears as well as our hopes—such acts we find constricting and not bourgeois, indeed quite unappealing. Prayers and songs and rituals such as lighting candles, distributing bread, kneeling, and embracing are quickly disparaged. The intellectual can easily dismiss them with a contemptuous smile and the observation that religion, even when practiced to a small extent, is a fraud.

We are afraid of the kind of experiences that challenge our sense of security. We are afraid to allow the petty bourgeois individual we were and are to be shaken and disturbed by such experiences. And that is precisely what religion does. We want to prevent religion from doing this. We do not want religion to do what its most radical critic says it has done and in spite of his criticism still does—protest and comfort. We are afraid of religion's inherent radical protest against the death-ridden life we live and cultivate. We do not want to hear the protest and outcry that religion raises. So we say that religion is not an outcry of protest but the babbling of addicts or, as Marx put it, the opiate of the masses. Actually, however, Marx knew full well that religion is an outcry of protest. And we can know that we are afraid of religion because we are afraid of the absolute demands religion lays upon us. We refuse to recognize any absolute standard for our lives. In fact, the very word "absolute" is suspect and unleashes thoughts of relativity. We can look at anything from a number of points of view. We can even look at the effect of horrible weapons upon the flesh of children from several points of view. We refuse to accept any absolute standards for our lives because if we did life would be unendurable for us.

Critics of religion anticipated that ultimately religion would simply die out in liberated and enlightened societies. Has this actually come to pass? The answer to this question is both complex and contradictory. In a certain sense institutionalized religion is dead. But it has not died in the ways expected and foretold by Marx and Feuerbach. They thought that religion would become superfluous because its promise of a meaningful life would be fulfilled. It was their belief that in the society of the future there would be no need for comfort or protest against the miseries of life because people would be really reconciled to their world and the meaning of life. Religion has largely died out in twentieth-century industrial societies—but its death has not been the kind that was anticipated. Comfort and protest were not rendered unnecessary because that which originally made them necessary had ceased to exist. Rather, they were rendered unnecessary by a deeper, manipulative destruction of needs. It is not that the conditions of human existence were so changed that the anticipated fulfillment was unnecessary, but rather that existence itself has become so differently programmed that "fulfillment," "meaning," and "self-realization" have become meaningless and incomprehensible concepts. Religion, which had become a useless instrument, was not replaced, however, by something better that would produce a real change. People simply discarded religion as old-fashioned and forgot how to use it, because their goals had changed. What strangled religion was production and the misuse of what is produced, and to that extent religion's critics were correct. But their prediction backfired. They did not reckon with the dialectic of enlightenment. Hope in the sense in which Feuerbach and Marx understood it must align itself in our day against their expectation that religion would die out.

Industrial society has excluded and rejected all truths that do not stem from economics. These noneconomic truths no longer have the significance of sustaining the culture because they no longer have any real impact upon how people live. Thus these truths revert to being personal, subjective, and emotional. They will continue to exist as the private pursuits of individuals, but what really is decisive and important in the world belongs to the economic sphere. People live exclusively for their work or, in their free time, for consuming what is produced. In other words, they live by bread alone. The old Marxist idea that through work men achieve not only a common mastery over nature but also fulfillment and security for the individual becomes increasingly questionable. The human depression grows!

Friedrich Heer speaks of a "great emptiness of spirit, with which we cannot continue to live without taking to ourselves new gods, charismatic but counterfeit gods." That place once occupied by faith in transcendent realities has, for most people, become an emotional vacuum into which the most varied emotions have crept and made their home—emotions that run the gamut from the most enlightened that religion can engender to the crassest forms of superstition. "I am no fool," a twelve-year-old girl recently told me. "I do not believe in God; I believe in UFOs." The false death of religion reveals itself in ways that are destructive.

In a recent documentary film a frail, elderly lady gave this response to an interviewer who at a crowded street corner asked her about loneliness: "I have been lonely for the past fifteen years, ever since my husband died. I do not want to be with people. They are no good." This woman's remarks contain more religious substance than any statements about belief in a higher being or life after death. Hers is the kind of talk one expects to hear from someone imprisoned in self, who accepts such imprisonment as the normal condition of life. The attachment to one another person becomes a surrogate for all other human relationships, and where it becomes absolute and exclusive it is a perfect expression of the irreligion that otherwise dominates all of life. This elderly lady does not know it, but she is dead. She knows nothing of the religion that calls dead what is dead and speaks of pharisees as whitewashed sepulchers.[2] Such a religion simply does not exist for her. That kind of religion would be a protest against the misery of those whose lives have been shattered and razed to their very foundations. It would be the kind of religion that seeks to set free those who have lost all desire to leave the shriveled, lifeless world of self.

But because of our normal fear of religion we cover up this radical protest. When we dismiss religion as superfluous, incomprehensible, and prescientific—arguing in a way that reduces the matter under discussion to the level of our conceptual powers—we blunt our protest. We hinder its expression. We relativize it, limiting it to the confines of what can reasonably be demanded. Religiously speaking, when we relativize the protest we deny the one who judges. We have no interest in a last judgment. Indeed, the mythical idea of a judge who at the end of time passes judgment in such a way that all transgressions and omissions are brought to light and nothing is forgotten is an expression of protest that cannot be silenced or satisfied. How strongly and deeply those people must have felt whose minds conjured up the imagery of such a judgment! How earnestly and seriously they took life and the injustice done them! They hoarded up their grievances for eternity!

The irreligious spirit of our day does not attribute any social relevance to this earnestness for one's own life. It may be possible to explain the large number of grumblers in the world as being due to their loss of a unified and public protest against the wrongs inflicted upon them. The religious interpretation of injustice is a protest that cannot be relativized. So, in an obviously irreligious world, even radical protest is incomprehensible. The critics of protest quite properly denounced the student movement as "religious" and as a "new doctrine of salvation." If the religious attitude of radical protest is to be found anywhere in our world today, it is in the socialist movement.

In the nonreligious interpretation of life it is facts and the perception of facts that count most; explanations take a back seat. "Irreligiosity constantly entices us to think that only what is manifest is everything. Want to or not, we think positivistically

—in a broad sense of the word. Under present circumstances the religious interpretation is something that cannot be prepackaged but must be constantly pieced together out of the midst of irreligiosity."³ It is extremely difficult even for those who think along Marxist lines to extricate themselves from this pressure of the obvious. We are on familiar terms with what is visible, with empirical data. Everything that can become an object of perception is manifest and objective. Interpretations— and, formally speaking, comforting and protesting are nothing but interpreting—by comparison are ontologically without meaning even if one cannot dispute their occurrence. The only thing that matters is that which is perceived. "Never before has there been so great a tendency to hollow out the interpretations in favor of the perception as in our day. This tendency is inherent in all forms of positivism. And none of us can extricate himself from it."⁴

We are afraid of religion because it interprets rather than just observes. Religion does not confirm that there are hungry people in the world; it interprets the hungry to be our brethren whom we allow to starve. But we do not even want the comfort of religion because that comfort is not some perceived object. "We arbitrarily think of that which is available for interpretation in manifest and objective terms as though it were an object of perception. That which is interpreted becomes objectified. We measure interpretation by the rule of perception."⁵ And we measure comfort by the yardstick of psychic recovery and functional performance.

We are afraid of being comforted; we prefer a long, drawn-out inner decay, a religionless poverty. The only kind of person who can be comforted is one who recognizes that he is without comfort and stops hiding from the fact that he is unhappy and empty. To this extent religion addresses its claim—that it leads to blessedness, happiness, and fulfillment of life—to the empty and impoverished life that merely functions. When it is said that the prodigal son was dead but is now alive,[6] then comforting or coming back home both mean the laying bare of a lifeless kind of life in which we function like just so many machines. The comfort of religion presupposes the death of the old man who always knew how to help himself. It is of this dying—which can hardly be described apart from the language of religion and poesy—that we are afraid.

3

The Matter of Experience

We are afraid to give expression to our experience and to use the kind of language which can do that. We prefer to deny and repress our experience through silence rather than to be fleeced by religion.

For example, I myself have certain qualms about writing this book because I am reluctant to talk about myself. I am afraid of having a religion or of being taken for a religious person. I am afraid of appearing ridiculous. I became aware of how strong these fears are when a team of Dutch television reporters came to interview me. We had agreed to discuss the situation in Vietnam and what we Europeans could do about it. Within a very short time the interviewer steered the conversation to theological matters. The very term "theological" is a defensive term, a technical cover. He began to ask the kind of questions—religious and personal questions—which are not customary in my German homeland. Frankly, I became rather irritated at this turn of conversation and, caught up in the spontaneity of our exchange, I blurted out something I had been thinking about for a long time. What I said was to the effect that one can believe only after one is dead. "How can that be?" one of the interviewers asked. "Have you had this experience?" For a moment I was taken aback. I paused and then said, "Yes, it was in connection with my divorce."

It was not as though I had forgotten all about the camera. I began speaking with the four-man team and together we tried to arrive at a bit of truth, only truth that had been lived and experienced. If it had not been for the cameraman, who became quite involved in the conversation and also began to ask some questions, I would not have been able to do what I did. Our entire upbringing conditions us to repress our real feelings, not to talk about our deepest, most important experiences in such a way that our embarrassment at speaking about ourselves in a personal way comes to us quite naturally. While changing a roll of film the cameraman explained what television is and someday can be. He did it without using the jargon, without sticking to any prepared script, without limiting himself to what was already known and needed only to be put into words, without repeating tried—and tired—formulas that anyone could mouth. He used words such as "life," "mystery," "vision." Above all—and this he emphasized with gestures—he used the word "miracles." "There are miracles," he said. "We have to make room for them." Of course, I was inwardly quite critical of such romantic remarks, yet at the same time his remarks took hold of me. As I spoke with these men I was no longer some kind of an object to which they directed their questions. They were no less embarrassed than I, and they too had to overcome the same qualms I did. We had created a situation in which we could relate to each other in a different way. We discarded our denial of experience and decided to talk to each other in a different way right then and there. It is not easy to reproduce experiences such as these, yet such experiences are indispensable to all of us for they make us really aware of how far removed we are from the so-called normal world, the shattered world of normal communication and normal perception. Our ability to leave no room for miracles and to reject anything that is new or different is one in which we have been exceptionally well trained.

By reducing everything we do to some kind of means to an end, we impose upon ourselves a straitjacket of rigidity and conventionality. Oddly enough, we are not aware of this until at some point or other we break out of the straitjacket. At that very moment I rubbed my eyes in astonishment and realized that I had been dead, that the way I had acted toward other people was empty, devoid of all genuineness, depth, and authenticity. I had been wearing masks, playing out roles, going through the motions. I had thought I could handle this television interview in the same way I was accustomed to doing other things—like ticking off a list. Indeed, I had thought that I could avoid any risk of talking about myself. But it had not occurred to me that not to talk about myself would have made me do something worse—say nothing that was of substance. I had thought that I could talk *about* religion and theology. But one of the strange things about the language of religion and theology is that it does not permit itself to be used. The reason for this is fairly clear. It is not something neutral, a mere instrumentality. When we use such language simply for the sake of using it, the result is sheer nonsense, garbled communication. The language of religion is the vehicle of collective experience and it is meaningful only when it speaks of experience and addresses itself to experience.

Believe me, it was not easy for me to talk about my experience of dying. For me the experience of dying had the effect of tearing to shreds a whole design of life. Everything I had built and hoped for, believed and wanted, had been dashed to pieces. It was as though one who was very, very dear to me had been taken away by death. But the loss and separation occasioned by a marriage gone on the rocks necessarily involves the matter of guilt. One cannot escape the sense of guilt, of having forgotten or failed to do something, of having made a dreadful mistake that could not be soothed and calmed by some kind of belief in fate. It took me three years to overcome and come to terms with the suicidal thoughts and desires that filled my mind. It seems as though the only hope and desire I had was to die. It was in this state of mind that while on a trip to Belgium I visited a late-Gothic-style church. I realize now that "prayer" is not the right term. I was crying out. I was crying out for help, and the only kind of help I could conceive of or want was that my husband would come back to me, or that I would die and my misery would be over and done with. Then and there the Bible passage came to mind: "My grace is sufficient for you."[1]

For a long time I had a particular dislike for that passage. It had always struck me as a brutal statement that meant that nothing could ever change. Paul had asked God for the health necessary for his work, and God simply slapped this earnest suppliant in the face with that kind of answer. He who had health and strength and smooth going and all manner of good things for countless others had nothing for Paul except a word which not only did nothing for him but actually made his life even more unbearable.

I must have reached the middle of the tunnel of despair at that point. I had not the faintest idea what that theological term "grace" means because it had absolutely nothing to do with the reality of my life. And yet "God" had spoken that word to me. After I left that church I stopped praying for my husband to come back to me, although for a long time I did pray to die. Little by little I began to accept the fact that my husband was going another way—his way. I had reached the end of the line and God had scrapped the first draft of the design for my life. He had not comforted me as a psychologist would comfort me, with assurances that what I had gone through was to be expected. Nor had he offered me any of the placebos society usually prescribes for people in my circumstances. He slapped me in the face, knocked me to the ground. That was not the kind of death I had wanted—or, for that matter, the kind of life I had wanted. It was an entirely different kind of death. Gradually it began to dawn on me that people who believe limp somewhat, as Jacob limped after wrestling with God on the shore of the Jabbok.[2] All of them have died at one time or another. We cannot wish such a death upon another, nor can we spare another from experiencing it by giving some kind of instruction. The experience of faith can be no more vicarious than can the pleasure of physical love. The experience of the sufficiency of grace for life, and the experience that nothing—not even our own death—can separate us from the love of God, are experiences we can recognize only after the fact. Such experiences are not written down and incorporated in drawings and plans which we can examine and check during the course of construction.

Contemporary attempts to restate religion or to state it anew simply do not make sense unless they take into consideration the centrality of experience. Probably it is more proper to speak of "experience" as a concept-symbol, for the attempt to create a precise psychological or social-psychological definition that would allow the concept to become operational is bound to fail. A definition would, of necessity, contradict what is meant, sought, or sensed. Experience sets itself over against the empiricism of normality and the idealization of scientific learning in which the individual is reduced to a number, and over against "bending the knee to the altar of reason."[3]

It would be wrong to think that someone like Ronald D. Laing, the English psychiatrist, simply because he is important for the religious subculture must be hostile to science and its rationalistic languages. Laing sees experience as more real than the "normal" condition of man, which is one of absurdity, loss of self, and routine participation in crimes such as war and exploitation. The schizophrenic who has "experiences" of an inner world, even though he is not able to organize these experiences and relate them to each other, is superior to the "normal" person who is dead even though he still goes through the motions of living. "I cannot experience what you experience. Nor can you experience what I experience. As human beings we are both invisible. Each is invisible for the other. Experience is the invisibility of one human being for another—we used to call it 'soul.' Experience of the invisibility of one person or another is at the same time more evident than anything else. Only experience is clear."[4] But even this evidence, according to Laing, is destroyed because of the normal process of upbringing that conditions people socially to "regard as normal and healthy the total immersion in the farthermost time and place." The person who is deceived about the experiences of the inner world is crippled also in his capacity for interpersonal experience and perception—and hence enabled to participate as a matter of course in the extermination of other people.

It is characteristic of Laing that at certain points he—almost existentially—departs from the language of scientific learning and starts to talk about I and Thou almost exclusively. He drops the customary net of presupposition, thesis, and argument, and attempts to use another language—that of experience. Reimar Lenz has also published some writings that originated from the experience of the religious subculture and also attempt a new language.

> It is our experience, arrived at through the use of psychedelic drugs, that the everyday awareness of our civilization is only one of several kinds of awareness—a highly cultivated form of worry. . . . The religious underground remains the locus of spiritual-emotional experimentation in which the loss of ego can be tested in the hope of finding the self. . . . "God" is the name we give to that voice in us which summons us to go beyond ourselves. Proofs of God's existence are pointless. The only way in which God allows himself to be proved is through

the growth of our God-consciousness. God does not exist, but we want to go to him.[5]

One must be clear about the strangeness of such a statement in an academic, scientific, political, or ecclesiastical setting. It gives offense, not a series of arguments; it remains in discontinuity; its language does not inform or establish anything but rather invites and courts interest. This statement cannot be understood except in light of certain experiences. It cannot be communicable as would be the case in the language of scientific learning but rather, like all mystical texts, contains a certain esoteric quality. "We have always insisted on seeing for ourselves. No more secondhand goods. . . ." When one compares a statement such as this with some statement issued by the church or a theological pronouncement, one sees immediately that the statements of a normal awareness are completely devoid of experience. Churchly and theological statements are "secondhand goods," the sole concern of which is to delineate and preserve a system. Experience is something to be impeded. The openness that could lead to syncretism and self-articulation must be avoided.

We can make the realm of experience the critical question with respect to the statements of religions, theology, and church. To what extent does a statement speak out of experience to experience? Does it express experience and admit experience? To what extent do even biblical and Reformation statements offer us "secondhand goods"? A statement would be Christian only if it expressed our hunger for justice and for participation in the kingdom of God.

But what experience with the inner world is meant? "Immersion into the inner world and inner time is perhaps to be seen simply as an antisocial retreat, a deviation; it is sick, pathological per se, and to an extent discrediting."[6] When a religious question comes up in a group discussion it causes the kind of embarrassment and aversion that the mention of sex occasioned among our grandparents. We are ashamed to speak of our desire for a life that is totally fulfilled and unfragmented; we are ashamed and embarrassed to think of it and we dare to express it only in disguised language. To die and to live, to be destroyed and to begin again, to fail and to proceed with a wholly positive attitude—how are we to come to an understanding about the key experiences? What forms are available to us?

To reduce life to the matter of getting things done, all in the name of a practicality by which every thought and deed is either justified or condemned, makes one-dimensional persons of us all. By focussing on purpose it forecloses the possibility of everything that is not functionally productive, such as prayer, poetry, artistic expression, worship. Consistent with this inability to articulate one's aspirations is the acceptance of one other kind of speech that goes beyond everyday speech—namely, the language of scientific learning. Our only alternatives, then, are everyday language or the language of scientific learning. We can either express ourselves in tasteless banalities or we can express ourselves in ways which are scientifically refined but totally devoid of values, while we let language that is human, language that goes beyond the conveying of information to express the whole range of human feelings, disappear. Although thousands have had the same experience as I and have died upon the death or loss of another, there is still no common agreement about what it means. At one time the soul used the language of religion and poesy to express itself. But when society values only what is useful for getting things done and when the only serious communication about what is useful can be effected only in technical language, then the acceptance of this way of thinking destroys every other perception of values. Indeed, it even destroys us down to the point of what we wish for. Moreover, such a way of thinking destroys every kind of living community because the theological or politico-economic advantage of knowledge on the part of those whom the prevailing culture regards as better educated destroys the uncontrolled communication that proceeds not from knowledge but from wishes and concerns. If we continue to move in this direction we will create a clerical system similar to the one we theologians have just left—a system in which knowledge is still power—and we will come not one step closer to Jesus' way, in which the greatest power is in the hands of those who wish more strongly, who act and suffer, whose starting point is not theory but experience.

Reimar Lenz criticizes the everyday consciousness of civilization as a "highly cultivated form of worry" that in the main separates social from spiritual progress—an attitude which believes it can do without self-confirmation and finding meaning and which, along with the established religion, also regards religious needs as something belonging to the past.

"Everyone is enabled and called upon to decide to think each evening, to complete participation, meditation. . . ." Will this kind of religious experience, which holds a faith in the capacity of man not shared by the major churches and which goes beyond the forms and doctrines of the church, express itself in a way that is socially relevant? Will we learn to share experience with each other? In the following chapters I try to interpret various writings in a way that bares experience.

PART TWO

STATIONS ON THE INWARD JOURNEY

4

The Golden Bird

THE GRIMM BROTHERS

Once upon a time there was a king who had a beautiful garden behind his palace. In this garden was a tree which bore golden apples. Each day the ripe golden apples were counted. But the very next morning one apple would be missing. When the king learned of this he commanded that a guard keep watch over the tree every night. Now, the king had three sons. At nightfall he sent the oldest son to keep watch in the garden. But when midnight came the son could no longer keep his eyes open and he fell asleep. The next morning another apple was missing. The next night the second son stood guard, but he fared no better; on the stroke of midnight he fell asleep, and the next morning still another apple was missing. Now it was the turn of the third son to keep watch. He was prepared to do so, but the king did not expect too much of him. In fact, the king expected this son to accomplish even less than the older brothers. Nonetheless, the king permitted the youngest son to take his turn at keeping watch. The young man stretched out beneath the tree and kept watch, but sleep did not overtake him. At the stroke of midnight he heard a fluttering sound and by the light of the moon he saw a bird fly by. The bird's feathers were glittering gold. The bird perched on a branch and had just picked one of the apples when the young man shot an arrow at it. The bird escaped unharmed, but in its flight one of its feathers fell to the ground. The young man picked up the feather and the next morning took it to the king and told him what he had seen the night before. The king then summoned his counselors and all of them agreed that a feather such as this was worth more than the entire kingdom. "If the feather is so valuable," the king said, "then one is not enough for me. I must and will have the entire bird."

The king's oldest son set out, determined to find the golden bird by using his wits. After he had gone quite a distance he saw a fox sitting at the edge of a forest. He raised his musket to his shoulder and took aim. "If you do not shoot me," the fox cried out, "I will give you a piece of sound advice. You are looking for the golden bird. This evening you will come to a village with two inns opposite each other. One is brightly lit and all within are having a jolly time. Do not go in there. Rather, go into the other, even though it has a drab appearance." "How can such a silly animal give sound advice?" the oldest son thought to himself, and he fired his musket at the fox. But the shot missed, and stretching out its tail at full length the fox ran off into the forest. The king's oldest son went on his way and that evening he came to the village with two inns opposite each other. In the one there was dancing and singing; the other had a grim and dreary appearance. "Why, I would be a fool," the oldest said to himself, "to go into that dreary place instead of into this other one." So he went into the first inn and lived there in riot and revel, forgetting completely the bird, his father, and all the good things that he had been taught.

As time went by and the king's oldest son did not come home, the second son set out to find the golden bird. Like his brother, he too met the fox, and the fox gave him the same advice it had given the older brother. Nor did the second son heed the fox's advice. He came to the two inns and saw his brother standing at the window of the one from which sounds of merrymaking emerged. It sounded so inviting that he could not resist it. He went in and there he stayed, indulging all his appetites and desires.

In time the king's youngest son wanted to set out, but his father refused to give his permission. "It's no use," the king said, "he will find neither the golden bird nor his brothers, and if misfortune overtakes him he won't know what to do, for he is a helpless fellow." But the youngest son kept insisting and finally the king yielded to him. Once again the fox was sitting at the edge of the forest. Once again it pleaded for its life. And once again the fox gave a piece of good advice. The youngest son was a goodhearted fellow and said: "Don't be afraid, little fox; I'll not harm you." "You won't be sorry," the fox replied. "If you hold onto my tail I'll help you to get where you are going more quickly." No sooner had the young man done this than the fox began to run so fast that their hair began to whistle in the wind. When they came to the village the young man let go of the fox, and following the fox's advice he went immediately to the less imposing inn where he spent a peaceful night. The next day, when the young man set out again, the fox was waiting for him and said: "Now I will tell you what you must do. Keep going straight ahead. You will come to a palace with a group of soldiers before it. Pay no attention to them, for they will be sleeping and snoring. Just go into the palace and through all the rooms until you come to the room where you will find the golden bird in a wooden cage. Next to the cage you will see a magnificent golden cage. But do not take the bird out of its wooden cage and put it in the golden cage or things will go badly with you." After saying this the fox once more extended its tail, the young man took hold, and once more they raced off over hill and dale, hair whistling in the wind. When the young man came to the palace he found every-thing just as the fox had said it would be. The young man came to the room in which the golden bird was sitting in a wooden cage next to a cage of gold. In the room he found the three golden apples as well. Suddenly he thought how foolish it was to keep such a beautiful bird in such a shabby cage, so he put the bird in the magnificent golden cage. Immediately the bird let out an ear-piercing scream. The sleeping soldiers awoke, came upon the young man, and took him off to prison. The next day he stood before the king, and, having admitted what he had done, he was sentenced to death. The king, however, said he would not only spare the young man's life but give him the golden bird if he would bring to the king the golden horse which could run faster than the wind.

The young man set out sobbing and sighing, for where was he to look for the golden horse? Suddenly he spied his old friend the fox. "You see," said the fox, "all this has come about because you did not do as I had told you. But take heart, for I will tell you how to find the golden horse. You must go straight ahead and you will come to a palace. There you will find the horse in a stable. The stable boys will be there, but they will be sound asleep and you can take the golden horse without any trouble. But you must put upon the horse a saddle of wood and leather, not the golden saddle you will find there, or else things will go badly with you." Thereupon the fox stretched out its tail, the young man took hold, and they raced over hill and dale with hair whistling in the wind. And everything was as the fox had said. The young man came to the stable and found the golden horse. Just as he was about to put the saddle of wood and leather on the horse, he thought to himself: "A beautiful animal such as this would feel disgraced if I put on it such a shabby saddle instead of the better one." No sooner did he touch the golden saddle than the horse began to whinny so loudly that the stable boys awakened, laid hold of the young man, and threw him into prison. The next morning the king condemned him to death, but promised to spare him if he would bring the beautiful princess of the golden palace to him.

With heavy heart the young man set out once more, and to his good fortune once more came upon the faithful fox. "I should let you drown in your bad luck," the fox said, "but I feel sorry for you and I will help you one more time. Your path will lead you to the golden palace. You will get there toward evening, and during the night, when everything is quiet, the beautiful princess will go to the bath house to bathe. As soon as she enters, seize her and kiss her, and she will come with you. But do not let her say farewell to her parents or things will go badly with you." Whereupon the fox stretched out its tail, the young man took hold, and they raced off over hill and dale, hair whistling in the wind. When the young man came to the palace, everything was just as the fox said it would be. The young man waited until midnight, and when everyone was fast asleep and the beautiful princess had entered the bath house, he seized and kissed her. She said she would gladly go with him, but she pleaded, with tears in her eyes, to say farewell to her parents. At first he resisted her pleading. But she cried and pleaded so much that he finally granted her request. No sooner did the princess approach her father's bed than he awoke, as did everyone else in the palace. They laid hold of the young man and threw him into prison.

The next morning the king said to him, "I will spare your life if you will remove the mountain which lies in front of my window and blocks my view. And you must do this within eight days. If you succeed, you will have the hand of my daughter as a reward. The young man set to work digging and shoveling both day and night. But on the seventh day he saw that he had accomplished nothing and that all his work had been in vain. So he began to despair and lose all hope. On that evening the fox came to him and said: "You do not deserve my help. Nonetheless, go lie down and I will do the job for you." When the young man awoke the next day he looked out of the window and saw that the mountain had disappeared. Full of joy he hastened to the king to inform him that the task had been done and that the king now must keep his promise.

So the young man and the princess set out on their way and before long the faithful fox came to them. "To be sure," said the fox, "you already have the best, but you must still get the golden horse." "But how shall I get the horse?" the young man asked. "I will tell you," said the fox. "First, bring the beautiful princess to the king who sent you to the golden palace. He will be so overjoyed that he will be more than happy to give you the golden horse. As soon as he does, mount the horse, extend to each a handshake of farewell, but last of all extend your hand to the princess. As soon as you take her by the hand, pull her into the saddle with you and ride off. No one will be able to overtake you because the horse runs faster than the wind." Everything worked well and the young man carried the princess off on the golden horse. Then the fox said to the young man, "Now I will help you get the golden bird. When you draw near the palace in which the golden bird is kept, let the princess down from the saddle. I will take care of her. Then you must ride the golden horse into the courtyard. When they see you there will be an outburst of joy and they will bring the golden bird out to you. As soon as you have the cage in your hand, ride back to us, take your princess, and ride off." All went well, and as the young man was about to set out for home the fox said, "Now you must reward me for my help." "What is it you want?" the young man asked. "When we come into the forest," said the fox, "shoot me to death and chop off my head and paws." "That would not be an act of gratitude," said the young man. "I cannot grant such a request." Then the fox said, "If you will not do what I ask, then I must leave you. But before I go I will give you a piece of advice. There are two things you must not do. You must not buy gallows flesh and you must not sit on the edge of a well." And with that the fox disappeared into the forest.

The young man thought to himself, "What a curious creature that fox is to have such strange whimsies. Who in the world would want to buy gallows flesh? And I have never had the desire to sit on the edge of a well." The young man and the princess rode on and on until they came to the village in which his brothers had remained. There they found a great deal of excitement and when the young man asked what was going on he was told that two men were going to be hanged. As he drew closer to the center of the crowd he saw that it was his brothers who were to be hanged for all manner of evil deeds. The young man asked what he could do to have his brothers set free. "If you will pay a large sum of money, we will set them free," the people replied, "but why would you want to ransom such wicked fellows?" The young man did not hesitate for a moment. He paid what was demanded for his brothers' freedom and as soon as they were freed the four of them went on their way. They came to the forest where they had first met the fox, and because the forest was so cool and pleasant and the sun was so hot, the two older brothers said, "Let us stop here at the well and rest and have something to eat and drink." The youngest brother agreed, and while they were talking he, without thinking or expecting anything to happen, sat on the edge of the well. Suddenly the two older brothers pushed him backward into the well, took the princess, the horse, and the bird, and set out for home. "See," they said to their father, "we have not only brought back the golden bird but the golden horse and the princess of the golden palace as well." But while everyone at home rejoiced, the bird no longer sang, the horse refused to eat, and the princess just sat and wept.

The youngest brother, however, was not dead. Fortunately, the well into which he had fallen was dry and he had landed in soft mud and was not hurt, but he could not get out of the well. Once more the faithful fox appeared and scolded him for not heeding the advice it had given him. "Nonetheless," the fox said, "I will not desert you; I will help you again." The fox told him to take hold of its tail and hold on, and thus the fox helped him out of the well. "You are not yet out of danger," the fox said, "for your brothers are not sure if you are alive or dead and they have surrounded the forest with guards and given orders to kill you if you are seen." Now, there on the roadside there sat a beggar with whom the young man exchanged clothing. In this disguise he made his way to his father's estate. Although no one recognized him, the bird began to sing, the horse began to eat, and the princess no longer wept. The king was amazed at this and wondered what it could mean. The princess said, "I do not know why, but I am no longer sad; I am happy. It seems as though my true love has come." And she told the king everything that had happened, even though the older brothers had threatened to kill her if she did so. Then the king summoned all the people in his palace, among them the youngest brother dressed in the clothing of a beggar. The princess recognized him at once and threw her arms around him. Immediately the two older brothers were seized and put to death. But the youngest brother and the beautiful princess were married and the king named him heir to the throne.

But what became of the fox? Quite a while later the young prince went to the forest where he came upon the fox. "Well," said the fox, "now you have everything you could possibly wish for, but there is no end to my suffering. You, however, could help me." Once more the fox begged the prince to shoot it to death and to chop off its head and paws. This time the prince did as he was asked, and suddenly the fox turned into a man—none other than the princess's brother who had been under a spell. Now their happiness was full and complete as long as they lived.

Seeking, losing, and finding make up the central theme of many fairy tales. Although the particulars vary from story to story, this threefold theme depicts recurring stages of a life's journey. In a fairy tale everything that is inward or spiritual is portrayed as an object, a thing. By the same token every thought becomes an act. Love is symbolized in the hood of Red Riding Hood; hate, in the poisoned apple the witch gives to Snow White. Every feeling, inward impulse, and stirring, every spiritual experience of the soul, is depicted as an object or an act. The interpreter's task is to convert these objects and actions back into experiences of the soul on its journey.

The first stage of the journey occurs in a world that at the very outset is beautiful and perfect, a world in which nothing is lacking or incomplete. Yet this perfect world contains something that drives people beyond its confines and disturbs and disrupts the compactness and self-containment of that world.

Something is lacking or is perceived to be lacking in that world; something is lost or inexplicable. It is then that someone gets the idea of looking for or demanding something that is not "here." With that "this world" is put in question and proves to be inadequate. One just cannot be at home in this world. In "The Golden Bird" a golden apple disappears each night despite the watchfulness of the older brothers. The older brothers fail to prevent this disappearance because they are so completely at home in "this world." It is only the youngest brother who sees the golden bird, which is the symbol of another world. And it is he who finds the clue to the bird, the golden feather. When it is discovered that something is missing, then the paradise that "this world" seems to have been—the paradise that existed at the beginning in one's childhood—is destroyed. A yearning is aroused within us to search for something that is not in this world. The loss, which is the starting point of so many fairy tales and which happens under even the happiest and most fortunate of circumstances, cannot be set aright even in the fairy tales. At the very outset there is a life-threatening situation that compels the hero to set out in search of what is missing. Nothing that originates in this world can satisfy or still this quest. Absolutely nothing that can be manufactured or purchased can compare with the "golden bird" or the "water of life" or the "red flower." That which is sought simply cannot be manufactured or produced, nor can it be possessed or used up. Rather, what is sought has to "be experienced." Only a journey that takes the seeker far from home can bring him to the goal. He cannot stay at home. Even the two older brothers, who are firmly rooted in "this world," as well as the younger brother, whose father does not think too highly of him (that means he is not tied down to this world), are compelled by an inward drive to undertake the quest.

This quest is the yearning for the absolute. Man's wishes go beyond earthly fulfillment, beyond everything conceivable, and transcend all the limitations of time and space, gravity, and causality.

> Wherever I looked, O Lord, I always found something lacking: "wouldn't it be nice if . . ." If there was a beautiful form, it lacked grace. If the form was comely and attractive, it lacked proper company. And if the form had that, then I always discovered something, within or without, that the tug of my heart resisted. Secretly or openly I discovered that such a being was not content with itself.[1]

If we are honest with ourselves, who of us could not make the same observation concerning himself? Who of us would not agree that finitude is at odds with itself, "not content with itself," always driving onward? Whether one draws the Platonic consequence of loving only the absolute, or the Christian consequence of consciously accepting the finitude, the yearning for the absolute remains. "What demythologizing cannot negate is the experience that the wings of thought, if they are not clipped, will surely lead to transcendence, to the idea of a world in which all present suffering is abolished and the irrevocable past is actually revoked."[2] The yearning for the absolute—in the fairy tale the absolute is the quest for the golden bird—is "the experience that the wings of thought lead to transcendence," an absolute transcendence which, like the messianic kingdom, also includes the past. Horkheimer speaks along this line of the "yearning for a fully established justice. Such a justice can never be realized in secular history, for even if a better society were to replace the present social disorder, past suffering would not be rectified and the suffering in surrounding nature would not be at an end."[3]

Religion is to be found there where man's deepest desires and yearnings have been dreamed. By deepest desires and yearnings I mean those that cannot be fulfilled empirically. Horkheimer speaks of "man's need for a state of eternal, unending blessedness," a need which is apparent even among those moderns who reject the resurrection of the dead, the final judgment, and eternal life as dogmatic statements. This need itself cannot be relativized or made up for or destroyed.

Critics of religion (who at the same time must of necessity be critics of poesy, which portrays man's search for the absolute) take their stand on their belief in progress. They believe that science will put an end to man's countless and inexhaustible wishes because on the one hand it fulfills these wishes in a limited way, and on the other hand it also exposes them as illusions. The big question, however, is if it isn't just the very fulfillment of some wishes and hopes that makes man's thirst for a final fulfillment even greater. Indeed, research in the field of primitive religions and millennial movements teaches us that magical *and* real expectations continually evolve into wishes for emancipation from colonial rule *and* for a new identity, thirst for riches *and* justice, so that religious behavior cannot possibly be divided into spiritual and worldly components.[4] A purely spiritual part is just as unthinkable as a purely materialistic part. Ultimately, the questions of religion which develop into complex religious systems in the so-called higher religions become increasingly more comprehensive, and the claim they make becomes increasingly absolute and incapable of earthly fulfillment.

In order to make clearer what is involved I would like to remind the reader of the artist and the artistic method. Here, too, there is an absolute which cannot be fulfilled, a yearning for perfection, a suffering at having only a part, not the whole, the incomplete, that which is not well stated but which is always in the old language of the old man. All art involves the wish to go beyond what is to something more than this, more than all that is known.

"Nor eye hath seen, Nor ear hath yet attained to hear, What there is ours, But we rejoice, . . ."[5] The mystics had forms of speech that express just this. The desire for another language, a language different from our ravaged and defiled double-speak, is an indication of this yearning. In the Melanesian cargo cults this yearning is expressed by the introduction of new words (some of which are in Pidgin English) that are incomprehensible to the uninitiated. The yearning for the absolute is enkindled at life's boundary points—mortality, death, guilt, suffering. But it does not flourish at those points. It is specifically the happy man who in the very midst of a full and rich life is driven on in the quest for fulfillment. This is quite obvious in the fairy tale.

What meaning is there for us in "The Golden Bird"? It is that "this world" is not enough. Working and consuming, which are of the very essence of this our world, actually destroy people. Hildegunde Wöller attempts to describe the new religiosity in a modern fairy tale that builds on the basic structure intended here. Her fairy tale also begins in "this world," which is ruled by Melok the Great and Beautiful Supermarket. The father and mother serve and worship these gods. Every day the father goes off to Melok the Great and at evening comes home tired and grouchy. The mother goes shopping at the Supermarket and before she goes and after she returns she is upset and nervous.[6] Their children are afraid of this world, and just as they are about to take their place in this world they break out.

What is the golden bird? It is the enticement to another life. It is the quest for the absolute, the desire to be whole. The bird is the great *no* spoken to this world and all its fulfillments, the refusal to be fed by them, the refusal to die by bread alone. The bird is nothing extraordinary but is rather the ordinary wish of people that has been muted by human religions and poesy. By no means is it only the sons of kings who go off in search of the golden bird. That search is undertaken by shepherds, farmers, beggars, housemaids, the youngest sister, and above all the youngest brother, the one who is not an heir, who has no security, no expectations to live up to, and who, in the bargain, is not too bright. The feeling that what we have here is not everything, that it doesn't suffice, drives us out into the quest.

The second stage in the fairy tale is the exodus out of this world. For the other brothers this exodus is made easy. This is why they do not get too far. But for the youngest brother the exodus is difficult. No one helps him. Indeed, in other fairy tales all the hero has to take with him is a cake of ash and some stale beer. He is poorly prepared for the task and one expects him to give up quickly and go home in defeat. In Wöller's modern story the two children run away from Melok and Beautiful Supermarket as well as from their parents and head off in a direction filled with danger and difficulty. It almost seems as though the measure of danger and "dread" which accompany the flight out of the Egypt of Supermarket indicate both the journey's distance and its potential for experience. He who takes the most with him and leaves little behind, and therefore remains much the same as he was before, has less chance of finding what he seeks. He must wander and get lost and remain stranded in this world and be subject to its laws and ways. He who does not give up anything cannot find anything. If the example of the parents points out the way, and their help lays out the path, then there is the considerable danger that the exodus will be a failure. The hero will find nothing except that which he has always known—a nice inn, dancing and music, the worship of the strong animal and contempt for the weak. The brothers do not change their values, and their journey leads them to nothing they did not already know and have at home.

The third stage is seen in the red-herring trails along the journey's way, the apparent finding and the losing. Even on the various stations of the journey "this world" opens and extends its arms to us. The older brothers yield to the world of appearance. In other stories the brothers' counterparts are satisfied with the first thing that comes along. They are willing to settle for an old rag rather than hold out for a fine suit of clothing. They demand too little of life; they are satisfied with second best.

But not even the youngest brother is completely freed at a single stroke. He also errs and must prove himself by undergoing new tests because repeatedly he too seeks the goods and beauties of this world. He seeks to add a beautiful saddle to the golden horse, provide a golden cage for the golden bird. He too is attracted and captivated by the beauty of what can be made and what can be found. To find what is sought requires the complete renunciation of this world; compromise brings destruction.

In the modern tale the error is portrayed as a drug experience in both a positive and negative sense. With the help of drugs the two young people escape from a life of total bondage to working and consuming. Nonetheless, they still fall back into the same helplessness of dependence. Even political solidarity and a hippie commune cannot end the journey in this story.

Harassed by the police, the hippie group dissolves and the hero must go bumbling on his way. The basic ways of experiencing the world—as failure, as being left alone, as force—remain unchanged. One can criticize the modern story because it puts political and drug-induced experience on the same level, but for many who with the help of the student movement became politically active, the motivation simply was not strong enough to effect a basic change and the old cultural values continued to prevail. The exodus did not go far enough; the journey was prematurely interrupted; the search was abandoned.

There is a fourth stage that follows the varied frustrations which in this story can be designated as the inward journey. This involves first and foremost the absolute rejection of this world's values. The two young people in the story of Melok the Great and Beautiful Supermarket renew their search for the absolute which is symbolized here as Crystal and Flower. In that search they are aided by helpers who are old (i.e., by those not completely integrated in the world). The guru and the wise old woman in this Wöller story are what the fox is in the Grimm tale.

The inward journey leads all the heroes of fairy tale and legend to place their lives in jeopardy. This inward journey is what religious language calls self-denial. In fairy tales the experience of dying, which is integral to human life, is symbolized by beasts such as snakes or dragons that possess supernatural powers with which they threaten the heroes. The heroes are confronted with tasks that cannot be resolved by way of instrumentalities belonging to this world. The seeking and finding can succeed only where the methods of this world are rejected, indeed, where such rejection intensifies the danger that confronts the heroes. The rejection of such methods on the inward journey is portrayed in fairy tales under such images as sleeping. The hero sleeps during the peak of danger, and that is when the impossible task is accomplished. The rescue comes only in the moment of extremest danger.

The inward journey is not an indulgent wallowing in one's own emotions, as the critique offered in the name of enlightenment might suggest. This inward journey has nothing of a fantasizing nature about it. The myths and fairy tales that depict this inward journey make a clear distinction between its individual steps and the kinds of jeopardy that accompany those steps. The severest jeopardy in "The Golden Bird" appears when the youngest brother, like Joseph in the Bible, is thrown into the well by his brothers. This too is a kind of dying, an immersion and drowning of the old "I" which now becomes free. The Christian symbol of baptism signifies vividly this experience of dying and being born again. The changing of clothes is a symbol of denying and emptying oneself. The hero must exchange his princely garb for that of a beggar. This exchange of clothing is a complete reversal of experiences which were arrived at in the first rich and glittering step of the journey. All that went before is for naught, the farthest point is reached—going astray has become a finding of self.

The fifth and last stage is the journey back into the world. This is the "happy ending" that is characteristic of all fairy tales, but this term actually conceals what is meant. In a fairy tale salvation does not mean that the hero is transported into another world; the relationship of this world to the other, of the seen to the unseen, of what is known to what is new, is not the relationship of reality to an opium-induced illusion. This world is not replaced by another. Rather, it is changed through the help of the other world. The goal is to reconcile the two worlds. The punishment of the villains, which fairy tales relate with relish, has less to do with so-called primitive cruelty than with the social relevance of salvation. What is portrayed here is not a happiness with or without anticipation of justice. We see this most clearly in those fairy tales in which justice is not restored but is established already at the outset and in which an end is put to class injustice. The poor farmer's son, the tailor, or the soldier wins the princess. The other world, which the hero experiences on his journey, is necessary for him in order to find his own identity. But that other world is not a substitute for this world. One does not remain in that other world any more than one remains in this visible world. Without this journey mankind can get nowhere, and every attempt to be spared this journey destroys the very truth of the reconciliation which has been achieved.

It is characteristic of contemporary fairy tales that even though Crystal and Flower are found the way back remains open and the fairy tale does not fulfill its function. This is because our situation does not permit a reconciliation that is universally valid. Our situation cannot be depicted and told in story form because it has not found a social form of expression.

In the final sentence of her modern fairy tale Wöller expresses
this basic difficulty: "How the story ends is something each
must discover for himself." That is also the difficulty of this
book, in which I would like to deal with the inward journey
and the return journey.

It seems almost impossible to reconcile the two: the magni-
tude of the inward journey which we need for experience of
self, and the way back into the society of a world that can once
more be lived in. Inwardness and involvement are not com-
panion attributes in most people, for sensitive people are often
not communally inclined, and people who like to be communally involved are sometimes lacking in sensitivity. Prayer
and work, labor and contemplation (Roger Schütz) appear to
be compartmentalized into two worlds, and the experiences of
groups that try to do both at the same time are too meager or
too weak to be discussed. In this sense this book is only a
tentative pointer in the direction of something better, namely,
a book about the return journey that is more saturated with
reality.

Happiness—finding the way back—has no social form of
expression. Our modern fairy tales must conclude with endings
that we ourselves devise. The critical question with respect to
expression of the deepest human experiences, those which we
regard as "the inward journey," is the question of connection
to and with society. Even the so-called new religiosity is like all
other modern attempts at religiosity in focussing on the enrich-
ment of a fragmented subjectivity. Where are the really new
ways of living to match the extremes of self-surrender? How
can religious groups express themselves politically and make
themselves understood? How can we actually live out the unity
of spirituality and solidarity?

One of the inevitable temptations one encounters in writing
a book (or in preaching or teaching) is that assumptions replace reality, and one thinks oneself to be ahead of the times

simply because one recoils at resistance to these assumptions. We do not have enough experience to be able really to speak about religion. I cannot overcome that contradiction in this book; I can only articulate it.

5

Elijah on Mount Horeb

1 KINGS 19:1–21

¹Ahab told Jezebel all that Elijah had done and how he had slain all the prophets with the sword. ²Then Jezebel sent a messenger to Elijah, saying, "So may the gods do to me, and more also, if I do not make your life as the life of one of them by this time tomorrow." ³Then he was afraid, and he arose and went for his life, and came to Beer-sheba, which belongs to Judah, and left his servant there.

⁴But he himself went a day's journey into the wilderness, and came and sat down under a broom tree and he asked that he might die, saying, "It is enough; now, O Lord, take away my life; for I am no better than my fathers." ⁵And he lay down and slept under a broom tree; and behold, an angel touched him, and said to him, "Arise and eat." ⁶And he looked, and behold, there was at his head a cake baked on hot stones and a jar of water. And he ate and drank, and lay down again. ⁷And the angel of the Lord came again a second time, and touched him, and said, "Arise and eat, else the journey will be too great for you." ⁸And he arose, and ate and drank, and went in the strength of that food forty days and forty nights to Horeb the mount of God.

⁹And there he came to a cave, and lodged there; and behold, the word of the Lord came to him, and he said to him, "What are you doing here, Elijah?" ¹⁰He said, "I have been very jealous for the Lord, the God of hosts; for the people of Israel have forsaken thy covenant, thrown

down thy altars, and slain thy prophets with the sword; and I, even I only, am left; and they seek my life, to take it away." [11]And he said, "Go forth, and stand upon the mount before the Lord." And behold, the Lord passed by, and a great wind rent the mountains, and broke in pieces the rocks before the Lord, but the Lord was not in the wind; and after the wind an earthquake, but the Lord was not in the earthquake; [12]and after the earthquake a fire, but the Lord was not in the fire; and after the fire a still small voice. [13]And when Elijah heard it, he wrapped his face in his mantle and went out and stood at the entrance of the cave. And behold, there came a voice to him, and said, "What are you doing here, Elijah?" [14]He said, "I have been very jealous for the Lord, the God of hosts; for the people of Israel have forsaken thy covenant, thrown down thy altars, and slain thy prophets with the sword; and I, even I only, am left; and they seek my life, to take it away." [15]And the Lord said to him, "Go, return on your way to the wilderness of Damascus; and when you arrive, you shall anoint Hazael to be king over Syria; [16]and Jehu the son of Nimshi you shall anoint to be king over Israel; and Elisha the son of Shaphat of Abel-meholah you shall anoint to be prophet in your place. [17]And him who escapes from the sword of Hazael shall Jehu slay; and him who escapes from the sword of Jehu shall Elisha slay. [18]Yet I will leave seven thousand in Israel, all the knees that have not bowed to Baal and every mouth that has not kissed him."

[19]So he departed from there, and found Elisha the son of Shaphat, who was plowing, with twelve yoke of oxen before him, and he was with the twelfth. Elijah passed by him and cast his mantle upon him. [20]And he left the oxen, and ran after Elijah, and said, "Let me kiss my father and mother, and then I will follow you." And he said to him, "Go back again; for what have I done to you?" [21]And he returned from following him, and took the yoke of the oxen, and gave it to the people, and they ate. Then he arose and went after Elijah, and ministered to him.

The word "journey" is one of the oldest symbols used to describe the inward experiences of human souls. In a time when learning theories tend more and more to be reduced to a technical model, within the framework of which the conditions under which we can learn and experience are researched and put into operation, the idea of journey becomes a countermodel. Those who have tried the journey maintain that we cannot derive the experiences that are most important for life through a process of input-output. Even the optimal conditioning of our ability to learn does not help us. We do not "go the way" by ourselves, and whatever else is valid for all learning—namely, that we can master what others discovered much more easily, with less effort and more quickly than those who first learned it—is not exactly valid for us and for our life. It is not necessary to live and breathe mathematics for years in order to understand the Pythagorean theorem, nor is it necessary to travel to Venice to be acquainted with Venice. But we do need to make that inward journey. It isn't only Zen Buddhism that, as Arthur Koestler puts it, cannot be delivered in the form of instant coffee. What kind of a journey is it? Where does it lead? The poet Novalis said: "That mysterious way leads within." Now, two hundred years after Novalis, that way is blocked by an almost impenetrable growth of defensive prejudices and fears. The critique, however, is often no less irrational than the thing criticized. "Our world is so alien to the inner world that many people insist that the inner world does not exist at all, and if it does exist, it makes no difference."[1] I turn here once more to the efforts of Ronald D. Laing to relate the transcendental experiences that occasionally break through in psychosis to experiences of the divine.

Laing's significance lies chiefly in his sensitivity to the psychic destruction of the masses. Nowadays it is easy to dismiss the Marxist doctrine of the increasing misery of the masses under capitalism as a false prognosis. But as soon as one separates this Marxist doctrine from its purely materialistic and gross product-oriented basis and relates it to psychic misery, the doctrine takes on a meaning that is difficult to refute. The psychic misery of the masses is increasing, and an ever greater percentage of the population at one point or another needs to be hospitalized because a "schizophrenic nervous collapse has been diagnosed."[2] It is estimated that there are ten schizophrenics walking the streets for every one in a hospital. These facts are the background of Laing's work and they explain his radicalism. "We are all murderers and prostitutes regardless of our culture, society, or nationality and regardless of how normal, moral, or profound we regard ourselves to be."[3] Alienation and destruction are what is normal; so is being dead—that goes hand in glove with the denial of the inner world. Since it is not the doctors who teach their patients but the schizophrenics who teach their psychiatrists about the inner world, Laing bases his position on the experiences of a schizophrenic when he describes the journey to the inner world with such key terms as:

> from without to within
> from life into a kind of death
> from going forward to going backward
> from movement within time to standing still within time
> from earthly time into aeonic time
> from ego to self
> from without (postnatal) back into the womb of all things (prenatal)

Corresponding to this inward journey is a reversal described as the return journey—that is, the journey "from within to without," and so on—something that is notably lacking in religious, psychotic, or drug experiences.

The interpretation of this journey is a basis for many religious and poetic writings. The Scripture passage at the beginning of this chapter can be interpreted along the line of the categories set forth by Laing. The passage begins with Queen Jezebel's threat to Elijah. In the preceding chapter the prophet is portrayed as a militant hero who inspired the people to seize the prophets of Baal and who personally slew them. Now he is afraid for his very life. He flees from the wrath of the queen in order to save his life. But the story ends with the third verse, and it is at that point that the inward journey begins. Elijah sends his servant away so that he can be alone. Now, having escaped the external dangers, he subjects himself to other dangers. It is a way "from life into a kind of death." He wants to die, and his falling asleep in the desert is an attempt to commit suicide. For him life is no longer worth living. Loneliness, thoughts of suicide, and sleeping are the symbols of this inward journey from without, from the inhabited political world out into the desert, from "going forward to going backward," images that range from acting, running[4] and struggling, to sitting down, resting, and sleeping.

Sleep is a person's natural return into another condition, and in this sense we set out each night on the inward journey. We exchange our conscious condition for another, one in which we are helpless and unable to control life. We go back into an earlier stage of our conscious, adult existence. The motif of sleeping is repeated in verses 4 and 6, but here the motif of death is replaced. An angel brings Elijah something to eat and drink, awakens him, and says: "Arise and eat, else the journey will be too great for you" (v. 7). The journey—that is, the inward journey, which goes from movement within time to standing still within time—leads from acting, in which time presses on, to regression, which sets in after wandering off into the desert. Then another time begins, "from earthly time to aeonic time," from one condition into another, which in the Bible is repeatedly and symbolically indicated by the number forty. It is the time of fasting and silence, of being alone, symbolized by the desert, the uninhabited, uncultivated land that is hostile to human life. The holy number forty expresses the possibility of escaping from the oppressiveness of earthly time.

We are not, as our normal experience maintains, restricted to the rivers of time from which there is no return. There is an inner-time experience in which a journey of only a few hours can mean more than years of earthly time. It is into this aeonic, eternal (not endless but *qualitatively other*) time that Elijah plunges and in the course of this journey comes "from ego to self." He denies his ego; he covers his face with his cloak (v. 13), and this gesture of reverent awe means not only that he no longer just wants to see and not be blinded. It means even more —the drawing back of the individuality, the denying of the ego. It is a kind of death and corresponds to what Elijah says when he says he is at the end of his rope, "no better than my fathers" (v. 4), without hope in his people, without any prospects.

What is left of a person who has abandoned himself on the journey in this way and who in so doing denies the conditions of normality, who has let go of space, time, motion, progress, and the ego? He enters upon the last stage, which Laing describes as "from without to the womb of all things." Still, the taking back has not gone far enough; Elijah still looks for his God in those powers that count in this world: in power and strength, and in the elementary forces of nature that mock all human effort. Here storm, fire, and earthquake almost have the meaning of deities that possess might and power. They represent the temptation to interpret the entire experience, to which Elijah is on his way, from a heathen point of view.

But what does it mean when it is said that God speaks and is experienced? There are several psychological models on the basis of which attempts have been made to portray the human experience of God. According to Carl G. Jung this experience of God represents the third stage of the inward journey. After passing through the "personal unconscious," where the traveler encounters his "shadow" and his identification figure of the opposite sex (*anima* or *animus*), he arrives at the "collective unconscious" of a level inhabited by mythical figures such as an aged sage or the dragon, all of which, under such symbols as the well, water, or the exchange of clothing, play a role. Jung describes the third and last stage of the journey as a level of harmony, clarity, and light. According to Jung, the mandala, which appears to the one who has traveled, corresponds to a personal experience of God and has about it as much a threatening and destructive character as one which grants happiness and satisfaction. This ambiguity, which catches a person up in the direct experience of God, can also destroy a person, drive him mad, make him ill, or even bring him to ruin. For this reason Jung assesses religions as buffers that offer protection against this direct experience. Myths, dogmas, and icons protect a person from having his own experiences, and thereby possibly from the return journey as well. For example, Jesus and Mary are buffers against archetypal powers. Protestantism, which largely forgoes the business of images, myths, and rituals, does not offer this defense. It develops no language of experiences that have a humanizing, calming, understandable effect. God, then, cannot be expressed; he is speechless; his character is perceived as that of a supreme power who casts men down and swallows up all other experiences of himself. He is so far removed from mankind, so "totally other," that experiences of him defy the power of speech and description. Nonetheless, those who have experiences on their inward journey can relate these experiences only in a language that is neither normal nor comprehensible. From society's standpoint such people are mad. Most of them condition themselves to an inner speechlessness; they forego the possibility of a return journey.

In the passage under consideration here, Elijah experiences God in a double sense. First, he experiences God as the womb of all things, as the farthest point of the journey, as the still, small voice of calm which Buber calls a voice of a hovering silence. This experience contrasts with an experience of might and power, and is possible only after many steps on the long way of the journey. Second, Elijah experiences God as the lord of history who restores to him a role in the political affairs of his people. God is the farthest regression a person can experience, going beyond sleep, beyond death wish, right into the "womb of all things." But at the same time God is the uttermost point, the one who keeps building his kingdom to the end of the world.

In the story of Elijah, God is not some kind of an object that we recognize and know; indeed, the question of whether God exists is a diversionary tactic that leads away from both our inner and outer reality. If God *is*, as other objects that we recognize, see, and know *are*, then the inward journey would be superfluous. One could spare oneself the self-emptying, the self-abandoning, this kind of death. One does not have to abandon "this world" for the sake of the God who *is*, nor does one have to founder in it. Contemporary civil religion—the kind that equates Christianity with the capitalist system—needs neither an inward journey nor a return journey; neither does it experience danger. Within such a religion God is a symbol that guarantees order. Nonetheless, as we have seen over the last ten years, this symbol can be easily discarded without any consequence. On this level we can discuss at length whether there is a God, but Brecht has already rendered this kind of questioning obsolete when he advises the doubter to consider whether the answer to this question would change the way he lives.

In the story of Elijah a consciousness of God is raised other than the one current with us. There is indeed a God who must be experienced over and over again. We find him not in storm, earthquake, or fire, in the blind and furious powers of nature, but in our decision for him. If we look for him in the forces of nature, then we are looking in the wrong place. If we understand that religion is a major form of human creativity, then it is not the *fact* that we project our thoughts that is to be criticized. What is decisive is what we propose and view as the *content* of our goal and value. Is it power and strength and mastery, which are the contents of "this world"? And is the relationship to them like that of the authoritarian type of religion described by Erich Fromm?

Fromm classifies religions according to their concept of God and their anthropology. He proceeds on the basis of a definition in the *Oxford Dictionary* that defines religion as the recognition of a higher power, unseen by men. This power determines man's fate and lays claim to his obedience, reverence, and worship. At first this definition sounds rather neutral and unbiassed, but at the same time it implies certain value judgments. God is conceived of as "power," and the basis of his worship lies in the fact of his lordship over men. "Power" and lordship are the central elements of this type of religion. God is all-powerful, all-knowing, and all-ruling. Man's most important virtue is his obedience to God; his cardinal sin is rebellion against the Lord.

Fromm works out the characteristics of this type of authoritarian religion by contrasting it to another.[5] The religion of the prophets, of Jesus, and of Buddha would be only partially—and poorly at that—described by words such as "recognition," "power," and "claim upon obedience." The counterdefinition is: religion is the perception of oneness with the All, a perception rooted in the relationship to the world which is laid hold of by thinking and loving. The basis for worshiping God is not reflection but the moral characteristics of love and justice. The chief virtue is not obedience but self-realization. The worst sin by which man goes astray of his purpose is precisely the obedience to law, unthinking and loveless adherence to rules.

The most important distinction between the two types of religion is in their understanding of man. In the authoritarian understanding of religion man is incapable of recognizing the truth; he is a powerless, insignificant being which does well to perceive its nothingness and deny its own strength. In the humanistic religion, on the other hand, God is a symbol for human powers which man seeks to attain. Man is capable of truth and love, and he lives from the feeling of relationship with all other living creatures. His basic mood is one of joy, not care and guilt.

What is the point of distinguishing these two types of religion? Certainly not to verify historically any kind of typology. In most historically developed religions authoritarian characteristics are interwoven with humanistic characteristics. But the distinction offers us criteria by means of which to judge whether a religion enslaves or liberates, advances humanness or a contempt of man, whether it promotes in us an infantile comfort and a compulsive need for order, compelling us to preserve and repeat, or offers us a faith that holds fast in the face of destruction and enables us to change the world. The God of authoritative religion is one to be feared and acknowledged. But there is another means by which to experience God: we can let him come in to us not by way of our acknowledging him, whereby no one needs to cover his face, but by way of a union, a going back into him. Elijah "hears" the still small voice; he covers himself and leaves the cave in which he had spent the night. It is probably going a bit far to interpret this as a kind of birth in which the way from ego to self is completed. In each case, however, the one who comes out of the cave is different from the one who wandered about for forty days and nights. He has reached another stage; he rises up, goes out, covers his face, and speaks with God. He has reached the goal of the journey; God appears and speaks to him. In contrast to many other religious experiences that stress the inward journey, Elijah now begins the return journey into the world. The prophet's political mission is renewed; he does not bow down in worship, nor does he found a monastery on the site of his blessed experience. Instead, he finds the way back into and for the world.

It is a polemical simplification to interpret the inward journey as a flight from the world. To put it in terms of the journey, God is the farthest point of self-emptying that man can reach on the way from ego to self. The God of the Bible is the deepest regression we need, and at the same time he is the process of increasing justice. He stands for letting oneself go *and* exerting oneself, for the opened hands *and* the clenched fist. The goal of all religions is to reach this farthest point, to experience the deepest self-confirmation and yet to return, and to communicate the experience that we are a part of the whole. The false division of labor that specializes and polarizes into pray-ers and battlers is thus at an end, and we learn that our hands have a double use: to pray *and* to do battle.

6

The Practice of Meditation

But how does one come to the experience of the Whole, of being sustained and upheld? The intent of this book is not to offer better interpretations of the religiosity of others, or to observe it in order to help others understand it. By its nature, religious experience is intolerant of everything we call interpretation. For example, as a human being with sexual needs it makes quite a difference to me whether I simply read a book on sex and discuss it theoretically or actually sleep with someone. So also in religion, impotence produces a surplus of theory. Religious voyeurism is no substitute for inability to "use" God and to enter into experiences with him. Theories about religious experience, such as Laing's journey or Jung's descent into depth-consciousness, are merely tools, aids by which to test one's own experience. Each step of one's own is worth more than all the knowledge and insight of others.

But how does one arrive at such steps? Certainly not by waiting for the experiences. The inward journey is an exercise, something that is cultivated; it requires concentration and attentiveness. Above all, the inward journey requires the greatest sincerity of which we are capable. It entails a risk—the risk of shame if nothing is there, the risk of emptiness if one does not change as a result, the risk of one's own person—and this risk is no less than that encountered on the way to another person. For us moderns, perhaps, fear of being ridiculous in our own eyes is the greatest shame.

It is probably a comfort to know that the religious experiences of the journey are not restricted to a few exceptionally gifted people. These experiences have been present in the great cultures for hundreds of years and have been available to all kinds of people. Every Indian youth knew what it means to fast and watch, to be alone for days on end, and within the framework of these ritually prescribed observances he achieved his identity, for example, his name, as one who belonged to the tribe. Spiritual exercises have by no means always been a luxury reserved for the upper classes. The earliest Egyptian monks, who practiced incredibly harsh asceticism, which included fasting and living in caves or trees, were for the most part simple Coptic field hands.[1] Dhyana, the Brahman method of meditation, is defined by a modern Buddhist as a kind of glimpse into the "inner world" and is described in practical, rather mitigating terms. Be it meditating upon the deep subjects of metaphysics or the ephemeral nature of this earthly life, dhyana is concerned "with the practice of periodically withdrawing from the turbulence of the things of the world and devoting oneself to peaceful introspection into one's own consciousness and conscience."[2] Dhyana, then, serves as a "discipline of inner pacification" for everyone. During the 1960s attempts were made in Japan to involve taxicab drivers in Zen Buddhist exercises for a period of a month. It was believed that such exercises would help to reduce the number of traffic accidents.

The basis of all these individual steps on the journey to the forgotten wholeness is a total participation of all our faculties. A purely spiritual accomplishment that does not disturb our regular routines is difficult to envisage. The religious subculture lives from its new physical experiences: fasting, sleeping on the floor, abstaining for a time or permanently from alcohol and nicotine or from certain foods such as meats (the frequent eating of which in industrial cultures is something that indicates the highest social status), listening to certain kinds of music and dancing in an ecstatic fashion, or taking drugs. The very act of appropriating anything into one's own pattern of living and consuming is in itself an act of standing somewhat apart from the outer world which is so deeply ingrained in us.

Breathing techniques are the next step. Even, deep, and conscious breathing must be learned first, and chest breathing must be replaced by abdominal breathing. A sixteen-second rhythm of four-second periods of inhaling, holding one's breath, exhaling, and holding is one of the basics of yoga. One gets to know one's own body by controlling one's breathing. These techniques, known to many women from exercises during pregnancy, do not mean very much by themselves, but to most people in our culture their application is neither possible nor comprehensible. Most people will have the same difficulty I had with this, for in certain emotional situations such as stress, overly intense concentration, or anxiety it is not possible to breathe meditatively. One simply is not in the position to let oneself go and to concentrate on breathing. Nonetheless, one can sense that worries and cares seem to have their residence in the stomach.

Exercises of this kind compel us to learn a kind of concentration that is not customary in our culture. It is not simply a concentration of will and mastery in which one subdues that part of the "I" that is difficult to control. It is an attempt to concentrate and be relaxed at the same time. One lets go of oneself and gets a feeling of gliding or sinking. Such exercises can be used as a means of inducing sleep.

One can also incorporate words into the exercise. In rhythmic breathing one can say "The Lord is my shepherd" while inhaling, and "I shall not want" while exhaling. It is important to fit the words to the breathing rather than what we usually do, fit the breathing to the words. One will have to pause at several points in order not to break the breathing rhythm. There are conscious pauses in which one inhales or exhales. One can test and recapture his ability to bring into harmony once again his breathing and his thinking/speaking. Another exercise with language involves the use of a "mantra," a word or text which contains magical sounds that impart redeeming powers. Usually we receive words only with the head, and our concern is with the information these words convey. But the words of Psalm 23, "The Lord is my shepherd," do not convey information of practical value. Meditative rambling is an attempt so to receive the other voice with our whole being, body and soul, that it becomes our own. The experiences expressed in such a mantra we make our own. We enter into the experiences of others, just as one person enters into a relationship with another person. We internalize this experience, not in the ordinary sense of a blind acceptance of presumptions laid down by others but in the sense of a completely free and conscious volition.

Every ritual performed under compulsion and every unconscious sharing of myths that remain incomprehensible have a destructive effect; they have been used all too long as a means of achieving domination. The present situation of irreligiosity portrays a possibility in this context: whoever decides for meditation or association with myth and ritual cannot do so unconsciously as a matter of course. One must know what he is doing, for in a no longer traditional society the simple repetition of a myth that is not understood no longer says anything. Such a repetition is much like a compulsive neurosis in which the constant contemporization of the past by use of symbols does not liberate the sick. This compulsive neurosis is the fragmented picture of a private religion; the conscious practice of meditation, to the contrary, lays the foundation of a practice that can be made general.

But how can that be? If I say "I shall not want," then critique and contradiction come immediately to mind and lead me to discard this mantra as something that is wrong and impractical for me. Here compulsion can effect nothing. But it is also possible for me to catch up my doubt into the "I shall not want"—to inhale silently and repeat "I shall not want." My internal appropriation of these statements, then, is not blind acceptance or dictated by some external power. Rather, it is an expression of my yearning; while I . . . who do want . . . form these words . . . I remind myself of what I lack. The remembrance of my experiences and needs, my pains and defeats, belong to speaking with meditative breathing. I abandon myself, my restless movements and rambling thoughts, in order to commence a conversation with myself in another voice. I rehearse myself into the ability to hear a promise, and the most important texts are promises (empty promises, the Positivists say). I attempt here to meditate on a text of Lao-tse in rhythmic breathing:

> The great creative principle flows everywhere,
> To the left and to the right.
> All things that are depend upon it for their existence,
> And it does not forsake them.
> It makes no demands of its works,
> It loves and nourishes all things
> But does not rule them.

In doing this I notice that I cannot keep on speaking but have to pause frequently. During these pauses I breathe consciously. I seek to find out if a sentence or half a sentence can be spoken while inhaling or exhaling. I bore into the text and the text takes hold of me. The difference between me and Lao-tse becomes less. I "eat" the text and have the fantasy that if I were to place my hand on a sheet of paper my fingers would write the thirty-fourth saying of the *Tao-te-king*. I speak the last two verses five times in a row, then, slowly exhaling, I say the last verse, I don't know how often (I did not count).

What is going on here? What am I doing? What am I trying to say to the reader? Certainly the reader can find everything there is to be known about meditation and breathing techniques presented more thoroughly elsewhere.[3] I am just trying to give a name to some of my own experience, of which loneliness and language are almost always a part. I am trying to express them in a form that I can share. One does not have to be particularly sharp to understand why the last verse of the saying of Lao-tse has such a fascination for me. It lessens my difficulties with God as he is understood by Western tradition, a tradition which has been dominated by males. I could of course also appropriate that verse cognitively, by an objective wrestling with the text. But the breathing-speaking way leads me further. I make the text my own when—in the kind of syncretism taken for granted in contemporary religiosity—I add to it a gesture that belonged originally to the famed mystical sound *OM*. "All of that (with a circular gesture indicating the universe) is Brahman. This self (laying the hand over the heart) is also Brahman."[4] The inclusion of such a gesture is important; in fact, one can regard the speaking of the mantra itself as a gesture. What really matters is whether the appropriation of a text for myself is successful. In that respect I have learned the most from my youngest daughter. A four-year-old, she prays, "Spread out both wings," in her own way. She raises her folded hands, spreads the arms—her wings—encircles the threatened chicken (herself), and when she says, "So let the angels sing," she throws her hands in the air. (Has anyone ever heard an angel with the usual kind of arms sing?) So she produces the song out of its own conceptual content that is part new and part old. She does not play the specific role—as Paul Gerhard portrayed it in this hymn—of the anxious chick which seeks shelter under the wings of Christ the mother hen. My daughter fell in love with the song as soon as she discovered the gestures that went with it. She understands the call to be addressed to her and she herself becomes that powerful winged being, the singing angel, the joy of Jesus.

The purpose or sense of meditation is not to understand a text rationally but to make it one's own, to accomplish it. When the rationalist asks, "What is the point of this? What is the point of meditating and breathing?" he destroys the exercise. That does not mean that these questions should not be asked; they assert themselves as a matter of course. But another question needs to be asked afterward. Is the analytical, rational association with this world the only kind there is? Is this kind of association productive enough for what we need? Is the change that I experience through knowing really the change that I am looking for? When I hold to this kind of method am I not always tied to "this world"?

The late-medieval German mystics speak of a necessity for the soul to achieve a "departure" from the world, from the body and the self. This departure is nothing other than what Laing calls the inward journey. To set out on this journey means for us to go away from the familiar traveled roads of our association with the world, because all these ways of the world and our self are subject to the basic law of the age to produce and consume. It is not enough to change things. In his free time the sales manager of a shoe factory will not be able to accomplish this "departure" from the world if he were to occupy himself with Lao-tse in the way in which we are accustomed, because his experience of the world has conditioned him to look upon everything in terms of being saleable or of having no value at all. Capitalism is everywhere and in everything; we cannot escape it. Capitalism rules not only our economy and politics but our whole way of thinking. We think in terms of end result, of bottom line, of time as money. We even ask if there is not a *faster* method of meditation! Can't we learn more and produce more at the same time we are meditating?

It is of this kind of total dominance of society that we must think when in ancient writings we find the word "flesh." That word expresses the power of this world, a power which is irresistible because it is so deeply rooted in our nature. For us the irresistible and inescapable power is no longer nature but the society that has become second nature to us. We remain in the flesh and cannot get out of it so long as we cannot question within ourselves the presuppositions of our methods of production and distribution.

Meditative association not only with words or texts but with ourselves helps us to just such questioning. To meditate means neither to produce nor to consume. Nor does it mean to make oneself fit for further production and consumption—even if one could market meditation like everything else in this world. Whenever we try to make it serve a purpose, the practice of meditation destroys the "contemplation," to use a word of which the mystics were fond. If I contemplate a rose or a pond or a human face and ask myself the question that cannot be evaded on our level, "Why should I do this?" then in that very moment I cease to contemplate. I begin playing my old game of becoming master of things through knowledge and use. I make the rose, the pond, and the human face subject to myself; I use them as aesthetic or psychological objects. Consciously or unconsciously I select. The capitalist in me has won out.

Some young photographers have gotten the idea to give up taking snapshots and true-to-life pictures of people who are not aware they are being observed and photographed. They ask those whom they want to photograph to choose the pose in which they want to have their picture taken. They add a new dimension to the pictures and turn what formerly were objects back into subjects. But what do they do with a rose or a pond?

Can they still take pictures at all when they have recognized the context of knowing, mastering, turning people into objects, destroying them? Or, to state the problem another way, what is a photograph supposed to look like that wants to show meditation and not mastery?

Breathing, meditation, contemplation—these are all attempts of the soul to "make an exit out of the world, out of the flesh, out of all mental objects, then finally out of myself, that is, out of one's own will,"[5] attempts to make the dominant "I" smaller, to become "I-less," so that we can come to ourselves.

In these attempts we seem to be withdrawing from reality, closing the eyes, as the incantation chant of mystical contemplation puts it. In truth we are assuming another relationship to reality, one of wholeness, in which the selection dictated by our interests is shorn of its power. For this reason the kind of religious thinking that is purpose-oriented—I am meditating in order to have an experience of God—also destroys meditation. "He who wants to become what he is not must give up what he is."[6] The inward journey is not a little walk along which one becomes intoxicated by one's own feelings. It is a form of experiencing the self that breaks up the physical and mental circumstances which constitute our state of normalcy so that experience, "which used to be called soul" (Laing), is possible once more.

7

Deny God for God's Sake

"The ultimate cause of our salvation lies in becoming nothing, in putting off our self."[1] For this "I-lessness" (which is identical to the goal of Buddhist meditation) the German mystics coined the term *Gelassenheit*. "Go out of yourself and deny yourself" (Meister Eckhart) is the oft-repeated summons to the inward journey. Such an expression was the fourteenth-century equivalent of our "turn on, tune in, drop out." The word *Gelassenheit* has undergone a drastic change in meaning over the years, a change that has diminished the mystical and strengthened the Stoic overtones of the word. The word *gelassen* has come to mean apathy, insensitivity, coldness of feeling. Henry Suso (ca. 1295–1366), the German mystic of the fourteenth century, who though he was not particularly original or outspoken was a tender and sensitive man, used the term in a much wider sense to include the ideas of patience, self-denial, obedience, conciliatoriness, acquiescence, self-control, control of desires, surrender to God. The term is used in contrast to selfishness or whatever lays emphasis upon the I and the self. A person filled with that emphasis must learn first of all to surrender himself. Indeed, this is the most important thing he can learn. He must learn no longer to cling to property, health, comfort, labor, the fruits of labor, and the lusts of the flesh. What is attempted here amounts to a radical drop-out, comparable to certain phenomena of the drug culture, in which people reject the most highly cherished values of the age such as education and career, getting and spending, health and creature comforts, work and sexuality, and everything connected with these values. One must keep in mind the true picture, the countercultural point of it all, if one is to assess fairly the obvious misery of the new dependence and the ruin to which it leads.

Unless there is a radical negation of those immanent values to which the ego is enslaved, it is not possible to abolish all selfishness and to deny oneself. "All the love in this world is based on self-love. If you had denied yourself you would have denied the entire world."[2] In the thinking of the German mystics we can distinguish three steps in the denial of self. The first step is to deny the world, which is also called the flesh. But at the same time this denial threatens the ego, its will and its relationships. I must also deny myself; that is the second step. I must be able to go away from myself and not worry about it. I must not cling to anything, not even to my own feelings, especially feelings of depression—and the mystics knew a great deal about such feelings. In this sense the expression "I am dependent upon God" has a deep meaning. I do not need to cling to these things because I myself am held fast. I do not need to carry a burden because I myself am carried. I can go away from myself and deny myself. To be able to surrender myself means that I can die. Thus, I go "from life into a kind of death"; I can overcome the deepest narcissism, which, according to Freud, consists of unconsciously denying the reality of our own death and being persuaded of our own immortality.

Gelassenheit in this sense includes the steps of the inward journey which Laing depicts. The letter of an unknown "friend of God," dating from the fourteenth century, says:

The loving soul must leave [i.e., go from without to within] the world, the flesh, and sensual objects [from going forward to going backward] and then go out of oneself and one's own will [from life into a kind of death]. Only then is the soul prepared to hear all the works of love done by our Lord Jesus Christ [from temporal emotion to temporal standstill]. This is the "still small voice of calm" that Elijah heard after he had been driven into God [from earthly time into aeonic time], and standing at the entrance of the cave, that is, ready with all his desires, to hear God's passing by [the self], yet with covered countenance, that is, the acknowledgment of his unworthiness [the ego], which made him properly humble and ashamed before the clear and illuminating glory of God [from without back into the womb of all things].[3]

The goal of the mystics is the birth of God in the soul. As with the Greek Fathers, this means that God's becoming man is in harmony with the idea of man's becoming God. What is novel about this idea is its revolutionary implication that became politically explosive in the Left-Wing Reformation. God can be born only in the soul that is "empty," that has cast out all selfishness and has gone from ego to self. "I live, yet not I but Christ lives in me."[4] He who has denied himself is on the way to becoming a Christ.

The third and highest step in the process of denial is that of denying not only the world and the ego but even God, the conquering One, the revealed God who promises salvation. "Therefore I beseech God to make me have done with him."[5] The mystics sought to extend the limits language sets upon communication, to shrink the sphere in which silence is the only possibility. To that end they made use of the forms of negative theology and of paradoxes ("Thou silent shout," "brilliant darkness"). Repeatedly the mystics were accused of heresy, of embracing radical views. That we should "deny" God for God's sake is one such radical thought. The meaning of such a thought is probably made clearer by Jung's assertion that religious symbols and words, the traditions about God, are

84

supposed to act as a buffer against the direct experience of God. The yearning for the absolute is communicated in the religions in a variety of ways: linguistic, social, mythical, ritual. At the same time this means that this yearning has restricted itself and put an end to itself. What once was faith has become a work, a pledging of oneself to someone. "So long as you do your works for the sake of gaining heaven or for your own salvation, that is, outwardly, things are not well with you."[6] The *Gelassenheit* which denies even God destroys this circumscription. The following anonymous letter is one of the greatest testimonies of mysticism in the German tradition:

> Learn to deny God for the sake of God—the hidden God for the sake of the unveiled God. Be willing to lose a copper coin so that you may find a golden one. Pour out water that you may draw wine instead. Creation itself is not so great that it can rob you of God or even of the slightest grace unless you yourself will it. . . . If you want to catch fish, learn to wade in the water. If you want to see Jesus on the shore, learn beforehand to sink in the sea! And if you should see the heavens crash and the stars fall, you will not be amazed. Not even God can take himself from you unless you will it; how much less the creation! Listen, behold, suffer, be silent! Deny yourself in broad daylight; behold with reason; learn with wisdom; suffer with joy; rejoice with longing; yearn with patience; complain to no one.
>
> My child, be patient and deny yourself, for no one can dig God from the depth of your heart for you.
>
> O deeply buried treasure, are you to be unearthed? O high-soaring eagle, who can reach you? O rushing fountain, who can exhaust you? O thou brilliant radiance, compelling power, simple turning, unveiled hiddenness, hidden assurance, single silence in all things, manifold good in single silence, silent shout—none can find you unless he knows how to deny you. Deny yourself, my child, and thank God who has given you such a dwelling place.[7]

In the mystical writings water is a recurring image for the depth into which the soul penetrates when it learns to deny itself. In the language of the mystics water and soul belong together. "O soul of man, how like thou art to water" (Goethe). Therefore the term "barrenness of the soul" as the mystics' term for the normal state of death is an especially menacing one. In myths people often find their partners after a long, uncertain, and dangerous sea voyage. Theseus finds Ariadne, Gunther finds Brunhild, and Tristan finds Isolde after just such voyages. This happens only after each of these persons has taken stock of his soul and penetrated into the soul's depths. The language of the mystics abounds especially in symbols of water. A person should "in deep *Gelassenheit* submerge himself into his very existence," the spirit "sinks into withdrawal," for God has become everything to him and "all things have become somehow like God."[8] A letter by Henry of Nördlingen puts it thus: "My wish for you is that you drink and plunge in the mighty waves of mercy."[9] Those who are in full possession of blessedness "are totally lost to themselves and submerge themselves into the divine will."[10] Thus blessedness is described as "submerging" or "swimming." "Often it seemed to him as if he were gliding through the air and swimming between time and eternity in the deep billows of God's unbounded wonders."[11] The term "submerging" is a central concept of meditation and derives from the language of mysticism. "I submerge myself" means that I have denied myself and can therefore sink or plunge or submerge myself into the depths of the sea.

There is a German children's Christmas hymn which in simple fashion expresses the secret of religion:

> I would immerse myself, O Lord,
> Completely in thy love,
> Present thee with my very heart,
> And all my treasure's hoard.[12]

Only he who is submerged finds life. Only he who does something totally and completely is truly human. We can call this secret the "great dedication," and a child can catch a glimpse of it because a child knows nothing of death.

The symbol of water can be understood only when one is aware of the danger suggested by water. Water means to go under and die. In the lamentation of one who is persecuted and despised it is expressed this way: "Thus the waters of much and varied sufferings overwhelm my soul and I am often stuck in the depth of the mud until I lose my very being. I come into a depth of the sea where dreadful storms seek to drown me. Then I cry with hoarse and weakened voice to Jesus Christ most true."[13] Here water is a metaphor for being in danger of annihilation. But it is only through such a threat, only through this death of the old man that the new man can be born. Only he who surrenders himself to this death of self-denial and self-surrender can find life. Christian baptism, in the days when it was administered to mature adults, was a ritual which expressed this truth. The old man is not simply cleansed in some moral way; he plunges deep into the unconscious. Jesus' baptism can be understood as a symbol of this: Man will survive the deep plunge into the unconscious; the waters will not hold him any more than they held Jonah, who is regarded as a symbol of Christ.[14] The threat simultaneously holds the salvation as well as the negation of the earthly self, the old Adam. But at the same time it holds the unending affirmation of the eternal self. We find the wish for submerging asserted in the most varied times and cultures.[15] Freud interpreted this wish as a regression. It is the wish to turn from the spiritual stage of maturity one has attained back into an earlier phase of our personal—but (if we follow Jung) probably also our collective—development. The deepest individual regression leads to swimming once more as an unborn child in the mother's womb. In the mother's womb everything a child needs is brought to it; the unborn child does not have to work, exert itself, or even stir. Going backward, we regress into this darkness of the womb; we seek warmth, darkness, and security instead of providing these things for ourselves as adults.

This interpretation, first of all of the mystical submergence but in a wider sense of all religiosity, is indisputable. It is only a question of how much worth we attribute to regression and how we judge it. This regression is worthless only to the dev- otees of "progress," the manager types who would even like to shorten or replace that regression which takes place during sleep. One can make the observation, however, that what comes out of deep regression is precisely creative accomplish- ment. It is not only artists, but scientists and academicians as well, who "find" important results rather than make them. In the Zen Buddhist skill of archery the only one who hits the target is the one who no longer consciously takes aim. Our culture denies the "values of the night" and goes to excess in illuminating everything; it destroys the rhythm of sleep and defames regression by such devices as shift work. But every- thing that grows and lives also needs darkness. Children look for a cave, a little corner in which to hide; adults build a church that represents darkness and warmth and the church is represented as ship and as mother in the church's symbols. The Christian Romantic poet Clemens Brentano illustrates this need for darkness in the lines

> O mother, please keep your
> Little child safe and warm;
> The world's so cold and bright.[16]

We can regard the critique of religion as an attempt to curb the human possibilities for regression and limit them to indi- vidual regression. Of course, sleep is still permitted, but not self-submersion. The individual unconscious is acknowledged and studied—as an unfortunate relic—but not the great col- lective attempts to practice and humanize regression as the religions do in their myths and rituals. Of necessity, then, the role of regression is undervalued, and regression is seemingly allowed only as a pedagogical concession to human weakness.

It is precisely at this point that the real questions raised by a progress-oriented culture are pushed aside: What is the relationship between regression and a progress that is worthy of the name? How much regression is necessary for mankind to be able to progress? How far must our inward journey go in order to effect external change?

The God of the German mystics appears to be a God who is purely regressive. Their fascination with the inward journey, of submerging oneself, is so great that it is often comparable to a fascination with death. They appear to hold no brief for the return journey, for the life that is supposed to be new, reborn. But this appearance is deceptive. Even Meister Eckhart was critical of pure regression. "For in truth, if someone presumes to receive more in spirituality, meditation, sweet rapture, and the grace of God than at his hearth or in the animal shed, then you are acting in no way other than as if you took hold of God, threw a cloak around his head, and tucked him under a bench."[17] Eckhart's verbal imagery summarizes the regressive tendency quite accurately. God is wrapped up like a baby, its head chopped off and hidden away in a hole. "For whoever seeks God in a certain way takes that way and overlooks and misses God, who is hidden in that way. But he who seeks God by no way grasps God as he is in himself, and such a person lives with the Son who is life itself."[18] Accordingly then, regression is an essential way by which to seek God, but regression dare not be made into the absolute, into God.

Even the practice of the mystics contradicts the idea that they held solely to mere regression. Indeed, many of these same people were also quite active as leaders in their respective orders who cried out against the prevailing state of affairs in their day and age. They traveled hither and yon, preached to great crowds, and labored as teachers and as physicians of souls. They founded schools and involved themselves in ecclesiastical and court politics. Some were even placed on trial and punished. Eckhart was one of these. Such activities always had political overtones and significance because the mystics offered their theology in the language of the common people rather than in scholarly or monastic Latin. This theology gave the masses a tremendous consciousness of their own worth: they could become one with God. And the mystics proclaimed this without mention of priest and sacraments. It is impossible to understand the many reform and sectarian movements of the late Middle Ages and their theological-political demands for the abolition of private property and autocracy apart from the theology of the mystics. Thus, the most radically heretical mystics, often called "free spirits," rejected the traditional doctrines of the church dealing with creation, redemption, and eternal punishment as well as the concepts of good and evil for those who thought they had attained perfection and peace through mystical oneness with God. Their return journey contained certain new ways of life and social changes; they rejected oaths as well as priesthood, sacramentalism, and private property. Likewise they rejected all forms of government that claimed to be based on greater knowledge, clerical ordination, noble birth, or masculine gender.

For them, contemplation and action, self-submersion and politics, and religious regression and progress constituted a unity. But for our understanding there is another difficulty that accompanies the mystics' understanding of God. Their writings speak of "loving God," "seeking God," or—in paradoxical language—of "denying God for God's sake." Turning to God always means turning away from the world. This sharp delineation between God and "the world," which permeates the entire body of traditional Christian (as well as Islamic and Jewish) thought, would be wrongly understood if it were understood in terms of time and space. Neither heaven nor eternity is played off out there against earth and life, even though this Platonic idea is what is suggested. Much more is meant by "God" and "world." What is meant is a direction of

will and of the existence of man. If they seek their life in con-
tented self-assertion, in holding on, in making oneself secure,
if they are bent on having, possessing, dominating, then that is
what tradition calls being "of the flesh" or "of the world." If,
on the other hand, the intention of life is dedication, self-denial,
and self-submersion, being instead of having, giving instead of
owning, communicating instead of dominating, then that is
what tradition calls "seeking God." This God alone, whom one
should seek, is not a separate heavenly person in a delimited,
metaphysical reality that would stand only in a negative relationship to us.

God means much more from a Christian point of view. To
put it simply, God always means "love" and world always
means "not love," which expresses itself as anxiety, detachment, security, "I-ness." In no case does the term "world"
mean human beings, what the modern age calls mankind; the
human being in this understanding belongs much more on the
side of God. When reference is made to seeking "something"
and not "God," this does not imply a distancing from one's
neighbor but only a distancing from whatever dehumanizes,
making a thing of a human being who no longer values other people but only the possession of things. The distinction between
"this world" and "God" is the attempt to draw human beings
over to the side of God. In this sense the following writing from
the pen of Henry Suso, who describes the depth of regression,
can be read and more easily understood if one experimentally
substitutes the word "love" for "God."

> You must set yourself free to the very depths of your being, to
> the unfathomable depths. But how? If a stone fell into unfath-
> omable depths of water it would continue to fall, for it would
> not touch bottom. It is in this way that a man must sink
> deeply and fall into the God who is unfathomable, and be
> rooted and grounded in him, regardless of what heavy burden,
> inner or external suffering, or even lack, which God for your
> own good often allows to overtake you. All of this should let
> a man sink even deeper into God, and in so doing he should

never realize his own condition or let it affect or worry him. Nor should he seek his own self. He should always keep in mind the God into whom he has sunk. He who seeks some thing does not seek God. All of a man's good intentions, his condition, and his mind should belong to God. To him be praise, the will, loyalty—never for us to exploit, or to be heard, or to be rewarded. Seek him alone.[19]

In a certain sense it is by this procedure that one comes closer to an atheistic interpretation that has a kind of basis in the thinking of the mystics. To deny oneself or to sink to the deepest level does not mean to enter into a special religious world or to demand a certain religious talent or to cultivate experiences. Suso relates a typical story from his experience. He found himself caught up in a rapture and had, he thought, denied himself, when a woman came to him to make her confession. He did not want to be disturbed so he curtly sent her away. But then God was no longer with him and his heart became "hard and unfeeling as flint." The woman had gone away with tears in her eyes, and it was only after he looked for her and found her and spoke with her that God came back to him. This is almost an antireligious story in the sense of a dialectical theology. Henry Suso tells it as an example that he had not really denied himself because he had "unwillingly withdrawn from the desire of his inward being," because he was trying to hold onto his rapture and therefore lost it. He could not yet deny God (i.e., here, his religious experience) for God's sake. In another important respect the theology of the mystics naturally contradicts the dialectic in a fundamental way because mystical theology does not regard God primarily as the "Lord," the mighty One, the alien God who is wholly other, the One who commands. Rather, the mystics regard him as the ground of endless self-giving who always appears—and not by chance —in the imagery of the sea. For the mystics, God is the deepest regression we need, and without the life-giving moisture of this regression we too become hard as flint. This regression assists us toward the achievement of our own identity.

PART THREE

THE PROBLEM OF IDENTITY

8

A Student's Letter

Please, hear what I am not saying. Don't be deceived by me. Don't let the face I make deceive you. I wear a thousand masks and I am afraid to lay them aside. Not one of these masks is the real I. Pretending is an art that has become second nature to me. Do not be deceived by it; for God's sake don't be fooled.

I give the impression that I am an affable fellow who has not a single inner or outer care in the world. I give the impression that confidence is my name and "being cool" my game, that I am a quiet stream, so in command of things that I need no one.

But don't believe me—please don't believe me. Outwardly I may appear quite confident and serene, but that is a mask I wear. There is nothing behind that mask. Beneath it I am what I really am—confused, afraid, alone. But I conceal all that. I wouldn't want anyone to notice it. If someone shows the slightest awareness of my weakness, it throws me into a panic, and I dread exposing myself to others. That is precisely the reason I desperately devise masks behind which I can hide. A clever slovenly facade helps me to pretend and to withstand the look of a knowing eye which would see through me. And yet such a look would be my salvation. I know it. If such a look were only one of acceptance or of love! That is the only thing which can give me the security I cannot give myself: the assurance that I really am of value and worth.

But I do not say that to myself. I don't dare. I am afraid to say it. I am afraid that your look is not one of acceptance and love. I am afraid that you will think ill of me, laugh at me. I am afraid that your laughter would kill me. I am afraid that deep down inside of me I amount to nothing and that you reject me for this.

So I play my little game, my desperate little game. On the outside I show a facade of confidence; beneath I am a trembling child.

I am rambling on! I'll tell you everything—which is really nothing—and nothing which really cries out within me. So do not be deceived by the things I say out of habit.

Please listen carefully. Try to hear not what I say but what I really want to say, what I need to say in order to survive, yet cannot.

I loathe this game of concealment. I detest this superficial game I play. It isn't honest. I wish I could be genuine and spontaneous, just be myself. But you must help me. You must extend your hand, even though it may seem to be the last thing I really want. You alone can take this empty glaze of death from my eyes. You alone can call me to life. Every time you are gentle and friendly to me, every time you encourage me, when you try to understand me because you really care about me, my heart takes on wings. Small and fragile wings to be sure, but wings!

Your intuition, your empathy, and the strength of your understanding breathe new life into me. I want you to know.

I want you to know how important you are for me, that you—if you will—can make of me the human being that I really am. How I hope you want to do it! Only you can tear down the wall behind which I tremble. Only you can tear away my mask. Only you can rescue me from my dread and insecurity—and my loneliness. Please do not pass me by. It will not be easy for you. My longstanding sense of worthlessness erects high, thick walls. The closer you get to me the more blindly I strike back. I resist with tooth and nail the very thing for which I cry out. But I am told that love is stronger than any thick wall, and I am counting on that.

Please! Try to tear down this wall with hands that are strong and firm, yet gentle, for a child is so sensitive!

Who am I? you ask. I am someone you know very well. I am everyone you meet, every man, every woman whom you encounter.

The author of this letter is apparently a student whose name is not known. Tobias Brocher tells how the letter came into his possession:

While I was lecturing at Louisiana State University a young man (I took him to be a student) came up at the end of a discussion and shyly laid a sheet of paper on the table. Nodding toward the sheet he said, "You probably will need this." With that he turned and walked away. None of us standing around the table knew him.[1]

The letter describes a basic identity crisis. According to Erikson, identity is developed during the stage of puberty-adolescence, when identity and confusion of roles confront each other. "The individual's feeling of ego-identity is the developed confidence that his inner identity and continuity correspond to the identity and continuity which others see in him, as this is attested in the tangible prospect of a career."[2] Without a doubt the writer of this letter does not have the prospect of a career. His own sense of "inner identity and continuity" and what he believes others see in him have fallen apart for him. He wavers between wanting to conceal himself and wanting to reveal himself, between masks that deceive and the real face that he seeks, between the outward "facade of confidence" which is supposed to suggest an affable, cheerful disposition, and the "trembling child" which he believes himself in reality to be. He speaks about himself in terms of his outward condition, in which he needs no one, and about the "empty glaze of death" in his eyes—that is the death by bread alone which is the theme of this book. And he waits with despairing hope that someone will see through him, set him free. "I resist with tooth and nail the very thing for which I cry out" is the same experience expressed by Paul two thousand years ago in the seventh chapter of his Epistle to the Romans.

What is the background of this crisis? I intend this question not in a biographical but a societal sense.

There are certain periods in history that are identity vacuums, when a feeling of alienation is suddenly abroad. Our age has this in common with that of Luther. His too was an age made up of corresponding elements: fear, aroused by discoveries and inventions (including weaponry) that radically enlarge and change the time-space perception of the world; inner anxieties that are confirmed by the collapse of existing institutions that the historical mooring of an elite identity had created; and the terror of an existential vacuum.[3]

What is an "existential vacuum"? This young man's letter expresses it well, not only in words but even more directly in the remarkable mixture of two styles and forms. On the one hand the letter is just that—a letter, a personal and direct pleading to a real "you" who stands in front of the writer. On the other hand the letter is a literary document of self-expression, the cry of one on behalf of thousands, as becomes clear at the end. The situational context of the letter is not indicated. The "you" of whom the author writes can give him nothing. Is the author really seeking help? On a second reading I instinctively ask myself if the young man had not often taken this letter out of his pocket after a lecture. . . . But this fantasy intends no denigration of the young man. The form of the letter, which in a certain sense is not at all clear, reflects an identity vacuum. The generalization at the end says only that which the writer, in the peculiar act of writing a letter anonymously and then disappearing from sight, has already expressed. This is not a matter of Student X and Professor Y. Is the "you" who is addressed here in any earthly position to fulfill the expectations? Is not the letter a religious document, a crying out to someone for whom we no longer have a name, someone who "hears what we do not say," who is not "deceived" or "made a fool of," a cry for acceptance? This becomes most clear in the "only you" at the end of the letter. Who is this "only you"?

At this point I must repeat what I have frequently stated before, because, as I see it, it represents the basis on which something such as theology can be pursued.[4] God has no ears other than ours; he can never be our alibi for withholding our love. When we do not hear a cry, even God does not hear it because he hears only through us. He has made himself totally and completely dependent upon us. For this reason the word "God" should be replaced in a meaningful way by such words as "love" or "justice."

In spite of this, and without giving up this basic thought of a nontheistic theology, I would speak to this young man if I met him (as indeed I do meet him every day!) about "God." I would try to restore to him something of that "original trust" of which he probably received too little. I could give him, if not everything, at least something. We can give the entirety, the whole, only in the form of symbols, earthen vessels. But what kind of an answer can one give the writer of this letter? What meaning do religion and faith have in the context of this question of one's own identity?

First, there is a deep and infallible security in "being of value," or, because that is the manner of speaking used by the dead, in the knowledge of being of incalculable worth. Faith is a repeated confirming of "ego-identity." Even the writer of this letter is of such worth that on his account ninety-nine sheep are left on their own;[5] on his account there will never be another flood; and on his account Moses led Israel and all of us out of Egyptian slavery. Religions speak of man in the highest terms. They speak of his responsibility and of his worth. By putting man into a relationship with the divine they establish self-worth, irrespective of how that may concretely be actualized.

One can understand this young man's letter as a crying out against the increasingly dominant understanding of man as a bundle of roles in which the chief function of the ego is to coordinate the various roles and to prevent these roles from colliding as disastrously as they might. In the framework of this behavioristically oriented line of thought the enduring human goal is the best possible fulfillment of prescribed roles. A change in the structure of roles, self-determination, the setting of one's own goals, and self-realization are all subjected to demands for accommodation. The question of meaning is replaced by that of functionality. Over against this the religions have in view another greatness and another peril of man who can "lose his life" despite the fact that he can function well. It is for this other identity that the letter pleads, and the writer has an idea that he himself is the letter and that living means to be read, heard, and used.

The author of the letter lingers much too long on the theme of facade instead of demolishing the facade. But simultaneously he articulates himself as a crying out, a message—and thus he shares in the greatest fulfillment of man, which consists in "needing God" and in becoming a message.

Reading this letter, I can only hope that the author will never become so old that he will forget the crying out which he once was. He is quite rightly afraid to grow up, because as a rule growing up means choking off this crying out and forgetting it. The young man resists the normal state of being dead, something that can be drawn out over forty or fifty years. It isn't enough for him to be born once. It is conceivable that someday he will cry out that no one can understand him anymore, that he is going "mad." But even that is endured in view of the threatening, normal nonidentity in which the disjointed parts—in other words, what he now is—mutually cripple each other. It is also conceivable that he will believe, and that means he will accept and affirm himself as a total person. "A person feels most himself when he means the most to others. In the last analysis a person is a symbol, a message, that receives life by being understood and accepted by someone. Faith can really say 'I' before God. It is through faith that all experiences, partial identification, and images of the past find their unity and continuity."[6]

But isn't this a cheap trick to play on someone who calls out to another person and is referred to God—the kind of trick that clergy play? We must try to say more exactly what the terms "God" and "faith" can mean. The writer of this letter speaks of himself as being a mask, a wall, as vegetating in a world of shadow. The "you" for whom he is waiting can tear off his mask and set him free from his shadow world, "breathe life" into him, and "make" him a human being. But this kind of waiting for help is like the waiting of a child. The encounters with other people must have failed because the writer must have tried to make these encounters into gods, and these gods simply had to fail him.

The offer which faith extends does not intend to prolong this infantility throughout eternity. To become an adult would mean that the author would no longer have to say, "Only you, O man or god, can tear down the wall behind which I tremble." Someday he will tear the wall down with his own hands. This is what it means to believe in God: to rise, take up your bed, and walk;[7] to be able to experience that "everything is possible"; to begin to live. The writer regards himself as weak, but behind that weakness is the strength of his crying out. He has been told that love is stronger than that wall. But what is love for him? In his present condition he can only receive love all his life, like a child into whose mouth a candy is pushed. He thinks he can experience love without becoming love. But "God" means to experience love by becoming love and to become love by experiencing it.

This letter calls out for God, not a candy kind of love. In a certain sense, God is already with the author, but, to use a figure of speech, it is only God's back that is present. Only his turning around is lacking. This turning around is difficult and causes dread because it represents a kind of death that no one can spare the writer. One must "have the right to go to pieces" and "the need to do just that is present in every one of us. We need unceasing renewal, a rebirth from the ashes of a passing condition of dissolution, death."[8] This right to "go to pieces" is denied to this young man in the normal world. This world has to deny that every living being has died more than once and that he needs this dissolution into ashes, of which the psychiatrist speaks, in order to be born again.

The child in the writer of the letter waits for the great miracle that someday will come and firmly but gently (so the child will not be so much as scratched) fetch him safely and unharmed from the prison. Therein lies the fear of being hurt, a fear that can lead to avoiding all human contact. But this fearful child must die. Each must give up this kind of seeking, waiting, hoping, and crying out. The new way will not be easier; it will be a way of waiting and acting, hoping and causing change, crying out and hearing. There is no guarantee of identity, and one must decide which is the highest goal: not to be harmed, or, to become love and not just receive it.

In all probability the author of the letter comes from the middle class and really does not have any pressing material need. In this respect he reminds us of the rich young ruler who came to Jesus and in his identity crisis "wrote him a letter."[9] "What must I do to inherit eternal life?" the rich young ruler asked Jesus. The question was a request for Jesus to take hold of him and take him along on his way. It was a plea to Jesus to tear down his wall. But Jesus did not tear down the wall. Jesus told the rich young ruler to part with what he had and then to come with him. This answer is twofold: you yourself must do something, and, a kind of death must take place. The rich young ruler remained behind the wall because he was very wealthy. The kind of death to which Jesus called him was not for him. He chose the death of normality. I know of no more dreadful story that can be told about our class. Is there any hope of rebutting it?

9

But When the Bright and Morning Star Arises

HENRY SUSO

Truly, O Lord, I find a great and total variation within myself. When I feel abandoned and forsaken, my soul is like that of one who is stricken, who has lost all sense of taste, to whom nothing is right. The body is limp; the mind is burdened; within my heart is hard and without I am sad and melancholic. Everything annoys and distresses me, even if it is pleasant and cheerful, for I do not know how I should act. I make mistakes quite easily. I waver and tremble in the presence of my enemies. I am indifferent and cold to everything that is good. Anyone who spends time in my company soon discovers that I am an empty house; the occupant of the dwelling, the one who formerly gave wise counsel, who encouraged and cheered, is not at home.

But when the bright and morning star arises in my soul, then all sadness takes flight; darkness gives way to light; the heavens are bright and cheerful and my heart laughs with joy. Mind and soul rejoice within me. I am filled with a holiday spirit and all that I am becomes a hymn of praise of thee. What before had been difficult, burdensome, tiring, and impossible—watching, fasting, praying, suffering, abstaining—becomes easy and pleasant. Everything that is difficult and demanding in life becomes as nothing in thy presence. Indeed, I am filled with a boldness that I lacked when I felt forsaken. My soul is so permeated with clarity, truth, and friendliness that it is no longer mindful of its former agony. I can look at things with a joyful, believing heart and without a sense of toiling. My tongue speaks confidently; my body takes on a quickness. And he who seeks it finds all needful and good counsel. It is as though I had transcended time and space and stood at the threshold of eternal blessedness. O Lord, who will vouchsafe to me the continuance of such a blessed moment? In the twinkling of an eye such bliss flies away. I stand there abandoned and forsaken—at times as though I never had known bliss—until, after another period of heaviness of heart, the moment of bliss comes once more.[1]

The above quotation from Henry Suso also gives an answer to the questions, Who am I? Where do I find my identity? The author describes two contrasting inner experiences, experiences which the American Negro spiritual "Old Black Joe" sums up in the words "Sometimes I'm up; sometimes I'm down." But what the song simply mentions is enlarged upon by Suso as two conditions of man.

It is easy for us to interpret such conditions in a reductionist fashion. For example, it is possible to interpret the sense of identity biologically as dependent upon hormones or one's age and vital energies. A moral interpretation is also possible: Isn't how I behave and feel a question of training, of will, of self-control? Both of these interpretations have a certain validity which we simply take for granted: In the realm of labor and production the interpretation in terms of the superego is accepted without question: I must do my duty, go to work, do what needs to be done, and do it every day regardless of my mood or the state of my soul. In the realm of subjectivity and leisure the interpretation in terms of vital energies is accepted without question: I expect that things have to go right for me, and if they don't I just make everybody around me feel guilty. As a result more and more people, if things don't go well with them or if they don't feel up to par, accept that fact as a matter of fate, as surely as they do their emotionally uninvolved functioning on the job. The interpretation of man in terms of the id (biology) and the interpretation in terms of the super-ego (the work-ethic) play steadily into each other's hands and the total picture is an essentially fatalistic view of man. The id and the superego are rigid and virtually inflexible. Work and leisure are both seen as coordinated with nature, and the moods that attend them are considered beyond one's personal control: I haven't the slightest responsibility for whether I am emotionally high or low—this is beyond *my* control—and while my mood can probably be influenced through chemicals or drugs, it cannot be controlled by me. Since identity is not a problem at one's work—after all, the other machines have no identity problem—neither is it in respect of leisure a serious problem that needs to be examined and explored and discussed. These forms of total self-alienation—in which my *self* is so totally foreign to me that I don't even *want* to exercise any influence on it—are something about which Suso the medieval monk knew nothing.

Suso describes identity and nonidentity neither as something that can be willed (superego) nor as something that is natural (id). Nonidentity he describes basically in terms of the absence of motivation. The statement "Everything annoys and distresses me, even if it is pleasant and cheerful" describes exactly the situation of most university students today. And the reason for that is equally contemporary: "I do not know how I should act." Because how one is to act is not derived from whatever is learned, "however pleasant it is," the diffuse melancholy that motivates one to do nothing controls us. We would be inclined to view this melancholy as something inward and would deny the dimension that Suso calls hardness of heart. Our self-analysis just would not go deeper than the melancholy. By comparison, hardness of heart is a matter of judgment—a devastating judgment. To be "as unfeeling as flint" is an image to which the dreariness of the soul corresponds, something that is arid and lifeless. This hardness, this kind of death asserts itself in all the dimensions of the ego: physical, psychic, and social. I "make mistakes," I am clumsy, I break, lose, or befoul everything around me. I am indecisive, that is to say, I am without any kind of decisiveness with respect to the political and social reality that confronts me. I see what was necessary only after it is too late. I am "empty," lacking relationship to other people.

Suso's description of identity, of the person who is at one with himself, also avoids the misunderstandings that are close at hand. It is not through willpower or conscious effort that I break nothing to pieces, but rather by "taking on a quickness," that I can overcome my shyness, that I can concentrate ("look at things without a sense of toiling"); the superego is not the cause of the soul's transcending itself. But it occurred to Suso in just this way to reason on the basis of natural tendencies, temperament, and physical strength. What he experienced goes against his nature, which is neither "bold" nor "quick." In any case, to become at one with himself means here to transcend the self as something that is already there. Natural tendency, training, and the course of life have fixed the ego fast— it cannot associate with people, play with children, sing, or dance. To achieve one's identity means to transcend this ego.

This quotation from Suso is taken from his *Little Book of Eternal Wisdom*, which was written sometime between 1327 and 1334. The book is written in the form of a dialogue between the "Servant" (as Suso called himself) and "Eternal Wisdom." The book contains a kind of practical, nonspeculative wisdom, guidelines in matters of faith and conduct. Suso is to be understood against the background of the basic fears and various forms of depression of medieval monasticism. Countless sermons and admonitions from that era deal with melancholy and seek to give advice and counsel against inward debility, and to give examples of people who overcame their depression.

Suso, for example, in one of his sermons, divides the inner weaknesses that drive people into corners into three groups: vague melancholy, disordered mournfulness, and violent doubt. These are the manifest expressions of the "Nonidentity" of that age. "Vague melancholy" consists of a person who, because of melancholy, is unable to do anything good without knowing what it is that he lacks. If he were asked why he was like this, he would not know what answer to give. Such a person is advised to contemplate the sufferings of Christ. The person with "disordered mournfulness" has enough perception to know what it is that he lacks, but he does not subordinate his feelings to God's will in that he takes hard what should not be taken hard. By "violent doubt" Suso means doubt of God himself and of his mercy, spells of opposition to God or his saints, and, finally, the temptation to take one's own life.[2]

It is important for one to be clear about this dreary background of medieval melancholy, of spiritual sloth and indifference, because only then does one understand what the identity of a person with himself means here, and with what harsh measures of ecclesiastical discipline these people struggled against the destruction of identity. What carried them through was the ability to concentrate, to see things. This ability was obtained by exercises in meditation: certain thoughts were rejected, even conversations about these thoughts were broken off with a single statement; other thoughts were suggested and offered to the person who was drowning in the depths of melancholy.

Above all, Suso made every effort to drive out of the melancholic's mind the thought that his depression was caused by some particular sin. Battle is waged against the kind of self-contempt that plays such an important role in the American student's letter. The threatening of identity by mournfulness in all its forms is the secret theme throughout this book as well. This threatening is neither naturalized, as in the physical interpretation, nor countered and resisted with the help of the superego, nor is it ignored and left to the psychiatrist, as is the case in the theory of roles. This threatening is understood as a psychic reality that directs us to an endless verification of our existence in a way in which a person cannot direct himself. Without this verification of the sense and meaning of our life we cannot have an identity. We can only live out our days by going through the motions of living, but without motivation. The ego power depends upon the closeness of God, of the "bright and morning star within my soul," the awareness that one is not forsaken and abandoned. In the course of the dialogue, Suso inquires how he can ever find the way out of his dilemma. "Eternal Wisdom" tells him that changelessness belongs to eternity, but that in the realm of time good days and bad alternate with each other. But the second argument is that God's presence is always there:

> [Eternal Wisdom speaks:] You allow your eye and heart to wander thoughtlessly about, hither and yon, and yet you have the precious and eternal image before you all the time—not for a single second does it turn away from you. You allow your hearing to wander when I speak to you many a precious word. You so obviously forget yourself and are so totally surrounded by the presence of eternal good! Why does the soul seek in external things that which is so mysteriously contained in the kingdom of heaven? [The Servant replies:] What does that mean, Lord, that the kingdom of heaven is within the soul? [Eternal Wisdom replies:] It means justice and peace and joy in the Holy Spirit.

From all of this the Servant concludes that Christ is present in the soul in manifold hidden ways which are "unrecognized by the soul" and that Christ likewise "draws the soul to himself."

What does it mean that the kingdom of heaven is *in* the

soul? Is the soul not totally independent of the rising and setting of the bright and morning star? That would be a mechanical misunderstanding. The basis of our identity is always most capable of being experienced by the soul; nevertheless, that basis is inwardly present even when we are caught in a web of a thousand external things and we do not perceive its presence. Our identity does not have its basis in the realm of what is visible or in that realm of past experience that we can call to mind. In this sense the "basic and original trust" of a little child, that "deep, almost physical conviction" which parents arouse in the child that "what they do is meaningful" and holds out "against the feeling of being robbed, fragmented into bits and pieces, and forsaken,"[3] is not a one-time experience that one would only have to pull out of some "inward" drawer. But in fact identity is rooted in the inner world of an assurance that goes beyond one's own Now-Consciousness. We can expand this consciousness and set out on an inward journey to this assurance. Erikson stresses that the budding basic trust in the one who is newborn can find historical-institutional security in an organized religion. Learning the language of a religion and performing its myth and rituals is one of the helps that society offers to the individual.

Suso calls the depth into which the soul can let itself fall "justice, peace, joy in the Holy Spirit." Let the soul enter upon it instead of waiting without motivation for the next outward sensation, and the soul will reach the depth and once more verify its identity. Then "the bright and morning star will arise in my soul."

The "bright morning star" is an ancient figure of speech for Christ.[4] "Of all the stars he is always closest to the sun; he never draws closer or farther away, and thus he demonstrates that whoever will draw near to the sun is supposed to be close to God at all times so that nothing can separate him from God, neither fortune nor misfortune nor any other creature."[5] It is clear that another star can take the place of this star, for example, some loved one, through whose closeness and assurance we are similiarly endowed with the ability to live with wings. The letters of the mystics are full of such religiously erotic experiences and none has the soul-destructive intention of neatly severing one from the other. The morning star informs of nearness to the sun; it rises in me so that I come into the same nearness to the sun and no longer have to accept as a matter of fate that "sometimes I'm up, sometimes I'm down" feeling. I remind myself of the experiences that have been had in the light of this morning star, and this reminding of myself is one of the important moments on the inward journey. Therein I obtain just a little bit of emancipation from the frustration I live with. In this sense all the essential biblical testimonies about man are not a description of man's just being here but rather testimonies to man's identity. When it is said that man is the "image of God," "son of the Highest," "master of the earth," "called to freedom," "perfect like God," capable of performing miracles, a being of freedom not slavery, of justice not oppression—all of these are testimonies of faith (rather, of a project!) in which the identity of man is derived not from what is already known about him but from the depth of his needs.

10

Who Am I?

DIETRICH BONHOEFFER

Who am I?
They say I step forth from my cell
Cheerful of heart and mien
Like the Lord of a manor.

Who am I?
They say that I speak with my guards
In a friendly and familiar way
As though they were my orderlies.

Who am I?
They say that I bear the burdens of the day
Bravely and with proud smile
As one accustomed to victory.

Am I really
What others say of me?
Or am I only that
Which I know myself to be?
Restless, melancholic, sick;
Like a bird imprisoned in a cage,
Gasping for breath,

As though being strangled.
Hungering for colors,
Flowers, the song of birds,
Thirsting for a kind word,
For the nearness of another person.
Trembling with wrath at arrogance,
And at the slightest offense,
Worried sick from waiting for great things,
Helplessly longing for friends,
So very, very far away.
Too tired and empty
For prayer, thought, work;
Drained and exhausted yet
Ready to take leave of all?

Who am I? This one or the other?
Am I this one today
That one tomorrow?
Or am I both at once?
A dissembler before all,
And before myself
A despicable, plaintive weakling?
Or is that which still is in me
Like a defeated army
Which yields in disarray
To a battle that is won?

Who am I?
Lonely questioning makes fun of me
But you know me, who I am.
I am yours, O God.[1]

Dietrich Bonhoeffer wrote this poem in July 1944 in Berlin, where he was a prisoner of the Gestapo. The poem was written about the same time as the famous letter of July 21, 1944, in which just one day after the unsuccessful attempt on Hitler's life, fully aware of his own impending death, Bonhoeffer eloquently stated the case for a "worldly" Christianity.

Bonhoeffer was only thirty-eight years old, but he was a man of character, decisive and clear in what he said and did. The mental images of an estate owner, a commander, and a victor, which are conjured up in the first part of the poem, speak for themselves against the background of the utter human degradation and humiliation suffered at the hands of the Gestapo.

Just as in the letter of the young student, here too an image from without and an image from within are contrasted with each other. The images contradict each other and raise the question of identity. But while the outward side in the letter of the student appears only as a deceptive facade, in the Bonhoeffer poem both images are correct. The social component of identity —I am that which others say of me—presses clearly and realistically to the fore. In a totally organized society the identity of the individual is basic to the social and legal order. The recognition of identity by society is essential. Here social identity develops into an unresolvable contradiction to the identity in which the ego recognizes itself. This identity is also realistically and objectifyingly expressed and attaches itself to such particulars as yearning for the song of birds, anger at the slightest offense. Linguistically Bonhoeffer stands completely in the classical and postclassical tradition, which stresses concrete things in general, that is, which speaks of colors, flowers, and birds and does not use the kind of words that would be much more descriptive and specific. Classical language is restrained, almost inflexible. Foreign and indigenous images are confronted with each other and subjected to the judgment of conscience. "Dissembler" and "weakling" are the result of this judgment. The coolness and harshness of association with oneself, the detachment that such self-judgment makes possible, become apparent. The reference to the "defeated army" or what is "still in me" seems to refer to death.

"The psychoanalytical meaning of the ego characterizes it as an inner-psychic regulator, the function of which is to organize experience and then to protect this organization against the untimely influence of drives and the exaggerated pressure of an overdemanding conscience. In fact, the ego is a very old concept that for the Scholastics represented the unity of body and soul, and for philosophy in general stands for the permanence of conscious experiences. In psychoanalysis the ego is nothing other than what it used to mean in philosophy: a selecting, integrating, continuing, and connecting agent that constitutes a center of the development of personality."[2] This formal description of the agent function of the ego applies quite aptly to the Bonhoeffer text, even though the ego portrays itself as tired, empty, and ready to depart this life. If one balances this from a negative standpoint with Erikson's portrayal, then the passive condition of the ego that is not at one with itself allows itself to be formulated as "ego weakness," helplessness over against driving wishes and the crippling of control and initiative. Nothing of this is conclusive for Bonhoeffer. Even in prison the forced crippling of initiative is organized and formulated. The "ego strength" of this identity also occurs clearly in the extreme inner strife of two mutually contradictory experiences. To be in control of oneself, to be active, to be related to a middle point—all of these essential attributes of identity remain intact. Even to be whole? The poem questions that.

Internal and external images behave in a characteristic way. A young man in quest of identity will often resist the outer image as counterfeit, masked, and superficial, and in so doing he will claim that he does not want to be what others see in him. He must build up the myth of unrecognizability ("no one understands me") in order to be able to grow inwardly without interference. All light falls within, into that which I know of myself. Within I am sensitive, open, and deep—all shadows lie without.

It is different with a total and mature adult such as Bonhoeffer. Here light and shadow are clearly seen and separated. The positive outer image is used in order to set one's own experience at odds with itself. The young man says: "I am more than I appear to be." The mature adult says: "I appear to be more than I really am. I appear to be stronger, more composed, less susceptible to attack than I really am."

What does this turnabout mean within the realm of a person's life? The myth of unrecognizability collapses when I am recognized or known (in Hebrew to recognize or to be known means something akin to loving, just as Adam "knew" his wife). It is in this process that I learn to communicate what is within me. I empty myself, and thus it happens that I know less of myself than others do, who experience my strength. The boundary between inner and outer image, which I have long defended, becomes increasingly open and can be forgotten.

Nevertheless, other situations develop in which the boundary line becomes more sharply delineated. One's own conduct is seen as an assumed conduct; assumed roles, such as being a mother, compel me to pretend that I have more strength than I have. If the compulsion and discrepancy are too great, then identity falls apart, as Bonhoeffer points out in the figure of the defeated army. But that does not mean that he understands a positive role to be only a role. He is in fact both—just as a woman can be a "mother," one who can always do everything, even while totally exhausted. But everything falls apart for him. The inner self experience makes him see himself as a "dissembler" in the eyes of others, and the criterion which the outer image gives him makes him classify himself as a "weakling," an expression of self-hatred. But the juxtaposition of both experiences remains, and questioning makes the self into an object to be played with. And that is a very serious game! There is no solution, and it would be harmful to see the conclusion as a solution. Whoever it is that I am remains an open matter. What is not an open question or in doubt is a certainty of identity that lies beyond questions and awareness. Even if I do not know and recognize myself anymore, even if I no longer understand myself, "God" knows me. "God" recognizes me and loves me. But what does that mean?

The psychoanalytical interpretation tends to put God into a relationship with the superego. But in Bonhoeffer's poem the rigid superego has already rendered its judgment ("dissembler," "weakling") and turning to God cannot be understood simply as an identification with a superego which has its origins in our childhood. If the word "God" here meant only the superego, then no help could come from him. The question is, Can there be any help at all where my consciousness is at an end? Can I do without knowing myself? Must I not have an awareness of my identity in order to be able to live and act? Of course! But obviously there are situations that obliterate this awareness. It is then that I must either give up my identity and, for example, begin to drink or in one way or another become a wastrel, a no-account, or I can still just "believe." "I am yours, O God" means: I do not belong to myself. My identity is not now dependent upon or a part of my awareness. I do not know myself. I "deny" all that: the images others have of me, which could sustain me, and the image of my own depression. Although Bonhoeffer is as far from being a mystic as it is possible to be, one recognizes in this point the truth of what the mystics meant by "go out of yourself" and "deny yourself." Bonhoeffer does both: he goes out of himself (whoever I am) and he denies both experiences—inner and outer, the relative self-certainty of outward mien and the relative self-certainty of depression. The second is more difficult, for it is easier to give up the false comfort of friends than it is to let go of one's own state of depression. But the "great submission" means that we also let go of our own depression.

I hesitate to use the word "submission" in connection with Bonhoeffer. I hesitate because too many take the word "submission" as something that applies only to women or mystics, whereas men are takers, conquerors, victors. Fromm says:

> Psychology can show us what man is not. It cannot explain what man is. The soul of a man, that unique core of existence, can never be adequately laid hold of and described. It is "recognizable" only to the extent that it is not incorrectly understood. So, then, the legitimate goal of psychology is negative: the purging of mistakes and illusions, not the full and total knowledge of the being of man.[3]

Now in the identity crisis of a person this single negative reference to the question "Who am I?" becomes clear. Under the best of circumstances all we know of ourselves is what we are not. Bonhoeffer overcomes whatever "illusions" and "mistakes" he may have made about himself. One can describe the course of his poem as a piece of negative psychology.

The fact that psychology has its limitations does not in any way mislead Fromm to a resigned silence.

> There is another way that leads to the uncovering of the secret of man; this way is not that of reflection, but of love. Love is the active penetration of another person by which the yearning to know is stilled through being joined to another. In this joining I know you, myself, everyone, and yet I "know" nothing. I know in the only way knowledge is possible for man, through being joined to another. Only loving can lead to the full knowledge that exceeds thought and words.[4]

Parallel to these two stages of human knowledge—of the negative, by thinking, and of the positive, by being joined to another—one can, with Fromm, distinguish two stages in knowing God. Theology is the first stage and it can at best be negative. A fundamental conviction of the mystical theologians was that it is impossible to make a positive statement about God. This position becomes clear when one has realized the unrecognizability of man. To recognize without being joined to the one who is recognized is nothing other than a form of submission and mastery. If in this way—that is, by making someone into an object—I attempt to know a person, then I can only destroy him. This is true of God. Maimonides said, "The more I know what God is not, the more I know about God." Out of this negative theology, the impossibility of knowing God, proceeds the mystical step of being joined—the mystical union. If by the processes of thought I cannot achieve the full knowledge of God, if the theology at best is negative, then the positive knowledge of God can be accomplished only through being joined to him.[5]

In his poem Bonhoeffer accomplishes this joining which exceeds thought. "I am yours, O God." Statements such as this are linguistically recognizable through simplicity, transition to the second person, address, and silence. More words cannot make the act of being joined to another clearer than it already is.

11

Psalm 139

¹O Lord, thou hast searched me and known me!
²Thou knowest when I sit down and when I rise up;
    thou discernest my thoughts from afar.
³Thou searchest out my path and my lying down,
    and art acquainted with all my ways.
⁴Even before a word is on my tongue,
    lo, O Lord, thou knowest it altogether.
⁵Thou dost beset me behind and before,
    and layest thy hand upon me.
⁶Such knowledge is too wonderful for me;
    it is high, I cannot attain it.

⁷Whither shall I go from thy spirit?
    Or whither shall I flee from thy presence?
⁸If I ascend to heaven, thou art there!
    If I make my bed in Sheol, thou art there!
⁹If I take the wings of the morning
    and dwell in the uttermost parts of the sea,
¹⁰even there thy hand shall lead me,
    and thy right hand shall hold me.
¹¹If I say, "Let only darkness cover me,
    and the light about me be night,"
¹²even the darkness is not dark to thee,

the night is bright as the day;
for darkness is as light to thee.

¹³For thou didst form my inward parts,
thou didst knit me together in my mother's womb.
¹⁴I praise thee, for thou art fearful and wonderful.
Wonderful are thy works!
Thou knowest me right well;
¹⁵my frame was not hidden from thee,
when I was being made in secret,
intricately wrought in the depths of the earth.
¹⁶Thy eyes beheld my unformed substance;
in thy book were written, every one of them,
the days that were formed for me,
when as yet there was none of them.
¹⁷How precious to me are thy thoughts, O God!
How vast is the sum of them!
¹⁸If I would count them, they are more than the sand.
When I awake, I am still with thee.

¹⁹O that thou wouldst slay the wicked, O God,
and that men of blood would depart from me,
²⁰men who maliciously defy thee,
who lift themselves up against thee for evil!
²¹Do I not hate them that hate thee, O Lord?
And do I not loathe them that rise up against thee?
²²I hate them with perfect hatred;
I count them my enemies.
²³Search me, O God, and know my heart!
Try me and know my thoughts!
²⁴And see if there be any wicked way in me,
and lead me in the way everlasting!

This psalm speaks directly to the matter of the identity of a human being. It is an answer to the questions: Who am I? What am I looking for in this world? Where am I headed? Where do I come from? What does my being here mean?

According to this psalm it is necessary to make a distinction between ego and self. The ego is world-oriented, entangled in subjective activity and rooted in self-assertion, and is the identity that is not derived from something that lies within myself but rather something that I experience as reality and to which I can give expression. I find identity, but I cannot create it. It is given to me just as my name is given to me. It is by my name that society recognizes me, and thus my social identity is something that is given to me. I do not live by my own strength; I am not autonomous; I am dependent. Of myself I would have no life worthy of the name, but with God I have life.

But what does that word "God" mean here? It is probably a good idea at this point to think back to what the mystics called "letting go of oneself," "letting oneself sink." Clearly the psalmist praying this psalm did indeed let himself go, let himself sink into the uttermost depths; yet he is actually borne and upheld, completely surrounded and enveloped, by God. One must put oneself in the psalmist's place and understand what he says from this standpoint, from what the mystics would call eternal blessedness, rapture, being overwhelmed, absolute certainty. If one does not arrive at this special perspective, then the psalm has no meaning. From this point of view the psalmist marks off all the dimensions of his life. But wherever he goes he encounters nothing that is strange and hostile. For him there is no longer any such thing as a chance event, as natural or social injustice which could rule forever; nor is there jeopardy or fear. In the midst of the world he is safely and completely preserved, borne, known, and loved. He has become transparent—his existence (v. 1), his mobility (vv. 2, 3), his mentality (v. 2), his language (v. 4), the entire area of his life (v. 3). And even though he finds himself in sin, error, danger, or misfortune, he is borne by the mystery of being secure (v. 6). He moves through space, heaven, and hell (v. 8), everything that is visible (v. 5) and conceivable (v. 9), day and night (vv. 9–12).

The experience of God is described by the paradox of shining darkness (v. 12). For him the universe is also the realm of the unconscious through which the soul wanders. Time and space in an earthly sense are no more; the soul wanders from postnatal to prenatal existence (vv. 13–15); past and future are interwoven with each other (v. 16). The psalmist who prays, whether he be asleep or caught up in rapture (v. 18b), is overwhelmed. He has experienced the grounding of his identity in God. He has left time and space. On his inward journey, which extends beyond all our normal possibilities of experience belonging to the external world, he has experienced not the coldness of the universe and the apathy of the whole toward an individual life but an endless confirmation of his self. The totality of the world, the farthest to which the minds of men can extend—and in this sense the word "God" is the farthest point to which language extends—contains an endless "yes" to all life. The human response to this "yes" that we perceive and hope for and seek, yet seldom experience in the way it is portrayed in this psalm, is the complete commitment and devotion that emanate from every verse of this psalm. It is like a much repeated amen—as Wolf Biermann puts it, "so it should be, so it must be, so it shall be."

The psalm is a journey to the inward world and to its most remote parts, its earlier time, and overlapping consciousness and unconsciousness. It is only on this basis that identity can be conferred and experienced, because identity is more than our temporal life, because our entire life is grounded in the mystery of the absolute. Who am I? The answer is: God knows me better than I know myself. He knows me in a way different from the way those around me know me. He knows me longer and deeper than any who know something about me. That means that my identity *is* more, *can be* more, than that which is already known about me. Scripture puts it this way: "It does not yet appear what we shall be."[1] It means that every human being is a mystery that is not swallowed up into social identity. Every human being is a mystery, something I understand only in union with God. To love, then, does not mean just to discover another person. It also means to realize the other person in his boundless depth, in his indestructibility —in the way in which God knows him!

Freud was correct when he said that religion is wishful thinking. Religion transports us to the depth of endless wishing. One of the most dreadful things that can happen to human beings is no longer to want to or be able to wish. Religious wishes (those that relate to the totality) are as peculiar to man as are his immediate needs. The language of religion expresses the need for communication that is neither restricted nor ruptured. Whoever regards this language as superfluous both minimizes and levels to the ground the all-embracing human need. He belittles us and destroys a basic form of human creativity. This is what we wish for ourselves: to be strangers nowhere, nowhere to be outcasts and homeless. "If I ascend to heaven . . . take on the wings of the morning . . . I . . . say, 'Let only darkness cover me . . .' "—there is no place in the universe where I could be lost or be a despised and unknown being.

But can we repeat this experience that the psalmist describes? Is it possible for us to pray this psalm? Can we believe as the psalmist believed? We cannot resolve this question simply on the basis of the text and its truth. Even if I can imitate the psalm and be in harmony with it, I am still not "contemporary" with the psalmist because two essential elements of becoming like him are lacking. One element we could call congregation or church or people. The other element that is lacking is indicated by the social consequences of the experience of such certainty.

According to Emil Durkheim's analysis, every religion possesses two indispensable basic components by means of which a religion becomes a social fact. These two components are myth and ritual. Myth is the story that is recounted, passed on, contemporized, and interpreted. It is within the framework of myth that society understands itself to be something above and beyond a mere collection of individuals. In myth, religion expresses its continuity and solidarity. It is through symbols and ceremonies that people express their feelings of dependence and of belonging together over against society. They gather together at regular intervals for exercises in concentration. The ceremonies performed at such gatherings effect a kind of rapture in which individuality is lost. The individual members of a group become a collective whole in and through "holy things." In the exercises of concentration this feeling of solidarity is renewed; the myth—later on theology—effects the portraying and shaping of the collective consciousness.

But we lack even this obvious reality of a fellowship. We have no language that is not delimited, no language in which truth can be so expressed that everyone—not just intellectuals —can understand it. We have no gestures that are significant to everyone rather than just to select groups. When religion is performed as myth and ritual, and this life of myth and ritual constitutes the background against which such a psalm (to be sure, as a piece of poetry composed by a particular individual) is received and accepted, then it is foreign to us who live without myth and ritual. Even if we mouth the psalm, we still have no meaningful context in which we can enact it.

A hitchhiker once told me that in Ireland drivers who passed him by made the sign of the cross at him. I do not know how, in a totally nonreligious culture, such passers-by could express their ties to today's beggars and vagrants. There are and always will be those material signs—a piece of bread, a sip of water, or an invitation to the nearest restaurant or diner. But what is happening here is less material in nature than it is spiritual. It is a bond which I can express—and even though I must get to work and the hitchhiker just wants to come a bit farther on his way, this signing of the cross is a gesture as powerful as the psalm because it issues out of a bond with the whole. This gesture excludes no one; it requires no previous judgment, no acceptance or rejection. It is a gesture that points to the totality of life while at the same time perceiving the identity of the individual. On the highway the hitchhiker is exposed to all manner of difficulty and danger; he needs help. It doesn't matter in the least whether the hitchhiker laughs at this gesture. What matters is that no one can be excluded from this totality.

This example is meant only to depict the essential condition of such a psalm if that psalm is supposed to be more than a piece of ancient literature. The psalm is supposed to represent and express the totality of society. But this very thing is difficult to conceive of, and in this regard nothing has changed since the time of young Hegel, who dreamed of the "beautiful totality" of the Greeks, and the time of Hölderlin and Marx. The social division of labor permits less and less of a common language. Not even symbols of a nonverbal nature are held in common, because the concentration exercises with myth and ritual, which would make these symbols self-apparent, are lacking.

That is one thing we do not have but need in order for us to receive such a psalm and allow it to be true for us. We just do not have a common situation to which this psalm would offer a common meaning. In this "godless" age it is only the cell group, the tiny circle of a fellowship, that can take the place of a common situation, circumstance, and language that all can grasp and understand. Conscious of the fact that we do not have such a common situation, this cell group speaks a language that is temporary, like a tent serves sojourners enroute to their destination. The wish for a language common to all, for gestures that can be understood by all, and for experience that can be shared and imparted can never be satisfied by these elementary gestures. Every kind of esoteric has this barb because the experience of unending security itself, as the psalm expresses this security, does not want to be simply an individual and group experience.

To this belongs a second basic condition, which is laid down for us by the appropriation to oneself of such a psalm: the consequences for social living. Positivistic irreligiosity does not pose a threat to the psalm to the extent that the psalm is something that is mouthed or prayed or believed. The threat posed by irreligiosity to the psalm is that—like the militant singing of "The International"—the psalm has brought neither consequences nor results. This positivistic irreligiosity simply reduces the psalm to a piece of private piety not at all unlike hobbies such as stamp or butterfly collecting. As long as the endless self-confirmation that the psalm expresses portrays a kind of leisure-time preoccupation with something that has neither consequences or results, the conditions for praying this psalm just are not fulfilled. Of what help would it be to anyone if he prayed all the psalms and found all the security and still did not change anything in his world?

The thesis of this book is that the utmost security of letting oneself go, of letting oneself sink, which we call by the ancient name of religion, is at the same time the greatest step forward. Because of the inner experience of the grounding of our identity, a return journey is necessary. Without this return journey the entire human enterprise of an inward journey becomes nothing but a means to the end of private comfort and self-protection.

12

The Wish to Be Whole

For a long time theology has failed to take religion seriously and to articulate and be sensitive to the religious need of men and women. It is precisely those enlightened theologians who took a critical stance toward their churches and traditions that are the ones who have neglected to make this need understandable, that is, to tie that need in with something which he who wants to understand can find again in himself. Many of us who talked a great deal about theology but were silent about religion were perhaps too much under the influence of Karl Barth, who condemned religion as something "merely human" and who made a radical distinction between religion and a faith based on revelation.

Possibly, too, we were too much under the influence of Dietrich Bonhoeffer's idea of a "world come of age" and were of the opinion that modern industrial society no longer needed such a thing as religion. We thought that society was able to resolve its problems rationally. Many were of the opinion that in an affluent society suffering and want and despair and yearning for a resurrection were to be found only in groups on the peripheries of society. I suspect that this opinion has already proved erroneous. But for too long a time the theologians have ignored the formulation of the question that religion makes necessary. The theologians were no longer in the position to perceive and to sense the "sighing of the oppressed creation" or to accept or articulate "the mood of a heartless world," as Karl Marx once described religion. The words "religion" and "religious" have been supplanted. They are felt to be embarrassing words. "Theology" or "theological" sounds much more enlightened.

So, then, the theologians gave the answers of theology without having listened to the questions of religion. These questions of religion, the yearning for something different, this wish to live differently, are not expressed in so many words or indeed even thought through. Rather, they are an uncertain feeling that can cause people to sink into dreams and divert them from reality. This feeling can easily be abused. But even this uncertainty and emotionalism is no reason to let the matter rest and to leave people to that "unexpressed" irrationality. The churches, too, bear some of the guilt that people cannot express themselves religiously. The religious institutions actually have promoted this inability by constantly providing ready-made, prefabricated expressions, terms, and words. So, then, it is hardly a wonder that the only way in which many people can express themselves religiously is outside of the church.

But what is this religious need? What is it that people are yearning for? It is the wish to be whole; it is the need for a life that is not fragmented. The old religious word "salvation" expresses this idea of wholeness and soundness, of not being shattered and torn into bits and pieces. It is obvious that those who have gone to pieces—and who of us hasn't considered himself one of these at one time or another—wish to be whole. At the same time, this wish is the wish for a life free of calculation and fear, without external, inwardized control of results and without risk. To be able to trust, hope, believe—all these experiences are tied up with an intense feeling of good fortune. It is precisely with this good fortune, of being whole, that religion is concerned.

As theologians we have spoken too little to this wide-ranging fundamental need because we often took the second step before we took the first. We have put the clear and certain direction which the Christian faith gives to this wide-ranging need into the foreground, rather than the need which is so difficult to put into words. We have not brought the provocation and the answer together. To use the language of Paul Tillich, we have not properly applied the method of correlation.

The wish to be whole remained stale and was seldom expressed in so many words. I consider this wish, this religious need, to be something that is indispensable even though it is extremely difficult to put it into words. Ernst Bloch calls what I have in mind "something which appeared to all in their childhood, but upon which none has ever entered: it is 'home.' " The yearning for home is the corporate meaning of the wish to be whole. Bloch's way of expressing this wish makes it clear how close religion is to sentimentality. But the fear of sentimentality is no reason to suppress this yearning for home. The fear of appearing to be unenlightened is no reason to mutilate ourselves in our wishes. The trouble, however, lies in the fact that Bloch is wrong when he says that something appears to "all" in childhood. Obviously there are social factors that so systematically dim this appearance that the great quest for home and hope which we call religion is never undertaken. I certainly do not need to emphasize that in my opinion this lack of the appearance of which Bloch speaks is a mutilation of people that takes bitter vengeance upon the present and future generations by the inability to wish, the poverty of expression, and the purpose-oriented enslavement to the everyday routine that admits of no transcendence of any kind.

We must try to clarify somewhat the conditions that lead people to something like faith and attempt to understand religion as a creative act in which people do what people in all cultures do: acquire a knowledge of the world, humanize nature, and overcome the alien, hostile god called fate. The religious need is the need to experience and to confer meaning. There can be no existence without this search for meaning. Precisely because I do not find that meaning and wholeness, but rather am frustrated and beaten again and again by meaninglessness and absurdity, by the uninterpretable, it can never be enough to understand myself as an object, as a link that is hooked into a deterministic chain. It is through a religious act that people set meaning over against meaninglessness, wholeness over against being fragmented, courage over against fear.

Obviously it is necessary for us to distinguish whether we are dealing with mere repetition of meaning that is oriented toward the way things are, or with new and alternative proposals of meaning. Without this quest for meaning even the category of the future would have to disappear because the future contains the possibility and promise of finding and realizing meaning. The mind is that place where reflection upon meaning and action hitherto achieved merge and make meaning apparent anew.

In this sense religiosity has been born out of lack, but only out of that lack which determines the real treasure of people. The nonreligious position involves a certain degree of resignation, insight into what it is possible to accomplish, that is, a submission to natural necessities. The person who has no religion is easier to satisfy. He is more "reasonable" because he has no yearning to be whole, to be unfragmented. The Marxist idea that the abolition of material need, exploitation, and oppression would lead ultimately to the natural disappearance of religion from the human scene presupposes not only a lack of understanding of religion but is itself an alienating curtailment of human reality that denies man's ability to dream, to express himself, and to realize his potential. The nonreligious mentality that grows out of this view justifies as reasonable only that which serves some purpose.

What people do in their free time, however, is not mandated by the idea that everything must serve a purpose. A society which demands that everything serve a purpose, ultimately destroys all kinds of human expression. Religion is made up of unrestrained wishes. It is creativity and expression, and for that reason religion, in the thinking of the prevailing system, is superfluous. It is characteristic of American sociology (e.g., Parsons) that it assigns expressiveness to the role of the woman and turns expressiveness into a thing. The man, who exhausts himself in the workaday world, which stresses practical results and production, is supposed to be regenerated by the woman, who represents a refreshing body of expression. In this system people's emotions are no longer communicated in a rational way. There is no longer a training of the feelings because these feelings are regarded as something natural but at the same time superfluous. The word "emotional" has been reduced to a derogatory expression.

This suppression of emotionality and expressiveness means that the feelings are bottled up and become a ready potential that can be exploited by the economy to incite a senseless sell-and-buy fever, and directly or indirectly can be exploited to serve fascist tendencies. Sorrow and good fortune take a back seat, and instead of these feelings a diffuse feeling of depression spreads itself abroad among people. The depoliticization of the masses also belongs in this context. The emotions are not expressed or verbally communicated, but these are the very feelings that religious groups with emancipatory tendencies can help set free.

The muting of expression is also the muting of hope for change. Religiously speaking, the god called Fate triumphs over the living God who speaks. The highest that men can hope for is favorable circumstances—something akin to winning the Irish Sweepstakes. But even these circumstances fulfill the purpose-oriented mentality that prescribes the highly developed technological foundation. Critique of religion as a critique of wishing is a mutilation of people to serve the interests of the capitalist or socialist purpose-oriented mentality. In our day this critique is objectively reactionary. That the word "God" may not be written with a capital "G" in the Soviet Union—but the names of soccer teams are written with capital letters—is a sign of this one-dimensional purpose-oriented mentality that destroys the power and desire to wish.

Every religious movement is an attempt to push back the boundaries of the absurd, and that includes the meaninglessly repeated, purpose-oriented mentality, in order to create a universe in which man can dwell.

The religious need is the need for experienced meaning, the yearning for a truth that has been promised and that is becoming increasingly visible. Religion is the attempt to regard nothing in this world as alien, hostile to man, a matter of fate, without meaning. Religion is the attempt to change everything that is experienced and encountered in all of life and to integrate it totally into a humane world. Everything should be interpreted in such a way that it becomes something "for us." Everything that is rigid should become flexible; everything that is chance, necessary; everything that appears to be meaningless should be regarded and believed to be true and good. Religion is the attempt to tolerate no nihilism and to live an unending and unrefutable affirmation of life.

As a variation of Freud's statement "Where It was, I shall become" one could say, "Where there was strangeness and chance and nothing, there shall be home, identity, and 'God.' " The word "God" then, no longer means a super-power dwelling in some world other than this, a world that intervenes in ours from without. Nor does "God" mean another realm, a heaven, another time after death, another kind of immortal, all-powerful being that stands over against us as a person. To be sure, we need the word "God" in order to express what we mean by the as yet unrealized totality of our world and the truth of our life which is yet to appear. In this sense it can be said that everyone has already decided over and over whether he believes in God or nothing, in the meaning of life or in total meaninglessness, by the way he lives.

Death is the most obvious limitation to the quest for meaning. Where freedom ceases, there the quest for meaning appears as despair. But meaning is also threatened by the banality of the everyday. The sheer repetitive nature of life also destroys meaning. Frequently when young people say, "I have no motivation," they are really saying, "I live in a world of meaninglessness in which nothing is worthwhile." One has to hear the religious question that this statement poses. The religious need is neither the quest for safety nor security that is conferred from above, nor is it a cheap comfort in defeat. The search for meaning is more extensive and goes farther than these reifications that themselves channel and reduce the need.

Because the complete meaning of life is something that is not visible or establishable (except, that is, for tearless eyes), religious need arises again and again from the lack of certainty; doubt and unfulfilled yearning accompany religious experience. The pain occasioned by this lack can be avoided only at the cost of religiosity itself: if we let ourselves be dissuaded from our religious need and are content with what is alien, hostile, and fateful in the world, and accept our own limitations as natural and destroy our capacity for transcendence. "Blessed are they who are homesick, for they shall come home" (Jung-Stilling). Man's greatest perfection is his deepest lack: the need for God.

This is a classical theological formulation that turns up in Augustine and also in Kierkegaard. It means that the wish to be whole is not the wish of an individual who is weak, frustrated, and of no account, and who regards himself as being of no account, but rather the steadily growing wish that issues from a life that is authentic and full. The greatest perfection of a person is also his deepest need: to need God. In other words, a person's needs continue to grow and there is no fulfillment that can satisfy these needs. The expression "to need God" states this yearning that will not be suppressed. The pain felt for the kingdom of God that is yet to be realized is, at the same time, a person's greatest treasure. This pain can express itself as one which touches on the whole and can be articulated only in a theological-political way. The destruction of the socialist hope in Chile, for example, is not only a misfortune that befell the "outer man" but also a destruction of a living hope we have gained from the confirmation of our being, which is what the inward journey means.

This book speaks about the general level of religious needs and for this reason deals with the inward journey. But the very question concerning how I attain identity, the question as to how I deny myself, is conceived of within the framework of the Judeo-Christian faith in which the accent is shifted from the inward journey to the return journey. The Christian answer to the infinite need is social and political. The meaning of the whole, the abolition of nihilism, the motivation for life are not found in an individual's absorption into God. Rather, the meaning is located in the interaction. The Christian answer to the question of meaning is that "God is love," and this general statement finds concrete expression in historical experiences of liberation. Faith as participation in this interpretation of meaning is an infinite affirmation that embraces all forms of life and gives them a unity. The more inclusive the affirmation the greater the closeness to people: solidarity is the most human expression of God's love.

Of course, this statement is subject to criticism. The objection can be raised that solidarity is not some kind of expression of something else, but that solidarity is solidarity and nothing else. But the reference to love for God should be not a proof but a rejection of every proof. Understood in this way, solidarity becomes an absolute value that gives a direct answer to our yearning for meaning and truth. As the "man for others," Jesus is the Son of God in precisely the same sense in which all of us are sons and daughters of God. We cannot relativize our cause by a purpose-oriented mentality. The struggle against misfortune purportedly meted out by fate, which affects a certain group, race, or class, is the continuation of Jesus' struggle. The least we can do is perform miracles against the injuries we find which are fatalistically accepted. We will be human beings; that is what we are promised. But only with each other! Solidarity is the Christian answer to man's wish not to be destroyed, not to be turned into a machine, not to live under the compulsions of monotonous repetition. Solidarity would be understood too narrowly if one attempted—from the course of history, for example—to derive solidarity in some scientific way and then to deny it to those who are not on the winning side. The term "love of God" indicates the wish of mankind for meaning and man's need for totality.

For our culture, Christ is the relevant symbol of the oneness of the love of God and of solidarity. For us to live as Christ lived—"to have this mind, . . . which you have in Christ Jesus" as Paul put it in Philippians 2:5—means the consistent refusal to worship anymore at points in our lives the god called Fate, which tells us that things will be as they have always been. Living as Christ lived means the inward journey to the emptying and surrendering of the ego and the return journey to the midst of this world. It means to learn to die and rise again. Instead of "rise again" we can say to undertake the return journey out of a kind of death into life. But what is the return journey?

I refer back to the story of Elijah on Mount Horeb. Elijah had experienced the stages of the inward journey up to the loss of ego and the finding of a new self, even to submerging himself in the ground of all things and to the experience of God in the "still small voice." But what happens now? Elijah does not withdraw into an act of worship; he does not make a pilgrimage to some shrine. Nor does he continue to divide things into the categories of sacred and profane, a division so dear to all religions. Instead, what happens is of significance for the Judeo-Christian tradition: the renewal of his political mission. Elijah does not linger in worship and ego loss. Instead he returns to the world. It's the return journey that is stressed in the story of Elijah.

A similar course is found in many stories in the Bible. The Ascension legend[1] depicts a fascination with rapture. According to Luke, the disciples see Jesus taken up into a cloud and disappear from their sight. They participate in this journey and are caught up to another place and time until two men in white approach them and say, "Men of Galilee, why do you stand looking into heaven?"[2] These words remind them that the Lord is coming again and impose a critique upon the religion of yearning. The disciples are not to stand about staring up into the heavens, but go to Jerusalem to set out upon the return journey.

The Bible's tendency to be critical of religion is unmistakable. But this tendency has little in common with the critique of religion that prevails among us because the Bible's critique takes place within a religious world. The biblical critique of the inward journey does not mean the transfiguration of a world that is understood positivistically. The critical question that biblical faith puts to human religiosity is the question of the possibilities of the return journey, not the simple recommendation to dispense with the journey entirely. Over the past two hundred years or so, bourgeois Protestant Christianity, while developing a kind of civil religion, has dispensed more and more with the inward journey. In theological reflection this has led to seeing the biblical critique of religion only as a self-confirmation of Protestantism's own inability to make such a journey. Clemens Brentano said: "A Philistine cannot understand that our Lord Jesus Christ died for us on the cross; he did not prefer to go to Apolda to build a hat factory." This bourgeois abstinence from religion, as though religion were a vile and dissolute thing, cannot justify itself biblically. This abstinence is an elite critique of religion and of popular piety that for a long time has preserved traces of the inward journey. This critique corresponds to the ideals of manly existence. The practical thought occurred first to the bourgeoisie to dispense entirely with the inward journey and to content itself with a return journey which is charitable and reasonable. The basis of this thought is that religion is a detour that, by a rational organization of the world, a person—at least as a male —can spare himself. One dispenses with the great detour of religion without noticing what a devastating effect this has upon people.

To dispense with the religious experience only increases the difficulty of an individual's finding himself, because the individual is at the same time dispensing with a consciousness of totality.

We must understand the desire to be whole and not fragmented as a basic and primary human need. The wish of growing love is to bind and join together ever larger entities. The individual wish to be whole is part of the wish to experience the whole and to be of its point of view, to recognize the creative principle. Christians express this yearning with the words "that God may be all in all." Not only should my life be fulfilled without the mutilation of my possibilities, but so should all life and the life of all. Jesus expresses this wish again and again in the recurring imagery of banquets and wedding feasts. All these are symbols of a joy which is shared in common.

The most bitter foes of the wish to be whole and to experience the whole are chance, detachment, coldness, darkness, and death. The person who lets himself go, who immerses himself in the sea of the unconscious, experiences not only that he is borne and sustained but that he is certain of the whole. Everything has meaning; justice and love are not merely ideas we have concocted, ideas which, if the occasion calls for it, can be replaced by others. They belong to the unconditional meaning of the experience of wholeness.

Goethe's friend Karl Philipp Moritz, in a book entitled *Anton Reiser*, tells about a pious old man who, in his last years, was of sound mind but feeble in speech. All the old man could say—and he said it repeatedly—was "Everything, everything, everything." He died with these words on his lips. This is a kind of formula for the confirmation of totality. "Everything" here means simply that nothing can separate us from the love of God; nothing can destroy us or take away the truth of our life. Everything belongs to us and is intended to be for us, not against us. The poet Hölderlin wrote, "What happens, let all of it be a blessing to you." This is the same kind of piety that affirms everything, omits and forgets nothing and no one.

This is how the attempt of all religions to include the dead into the one beloved reality is to be understood. The mythological basis of praying for the dead is rooted in the notion of purgatory, a place of temporary torment. Our praying for the dead is supposed to move God to shorten the time of torment and to relieve the suffering of the deceased. This imagery is not practicable for us, but, nonetheless, does this mean that our wishes for the dead are at an end? Can our love for one who is dead end with death? The religions have developed certain forms—rituals and theology—that express a continuation of human relationships that goes beyond the pale of death. The continuation of a society and the cessation of an individual depend upon this integration of the living and the dead as well as upon how radically "everything" is understood. Which mythological language one uses to appropriate "everything" is not decisive because every language that wants "everything" has a mythical character.

The two basic experiences of religion—totality and identity—continually need, as does all existential knowledge that is not finally possessed simply for having one day been acquired, a new portrayal, articulation, language. And although our knowledge of the totality is not certain, and our language, which no longer has a command of mythology, is inexact, and this attempt to express "everything" flounders, nonetheless it is absolutely necessary. We need a consciousness of the entire world, of a justice that is absolute and valid for all. We cannot rear children without passing on to them the experience of the whole. We cannot nurse incurables if we do not have access to this experience. We cannot wage passionate warfare against injustice and exploitation if we do not know that we are upheld and sustained in our demand for justice by the context of meaning of the world in which an authentic and fulfilled life is promised to all men.

The experience of the whole and of totality includes not only the dead but also the pains and sorrows of all the living. The liturgy calls to our remembrance the forsaken, the heavy of heart, those who weep, and draws them into the great "everything." The Christian accent on the return journey contains an affirmation of all earthly experience, even that of suffering, sin, and mortality. There is in this an inherent affirmation of mortality and suffering that is too difficult for us to put an end to because to do so would make us apathetic. Henry Suso said that in heaven the human soul will sing a song more lovely than that of all the angels because the angels have never suffered. The religious experience stands in danger of wanting to sing like the angels and to forget mortality and suffering. Where that is the case, the inward journey and the return journey remain separated from each other, just as they are torn apart in the prevailing culture.

At several points I have indicated the basic difficulty of this book. This book is incomplete because it is not possible to spell out the return journey under the current circumstances of the religious-political situation. In central Europe, at any rate, we have no practical experience that embodies the inward and return journeys. There is no lack of ideas, postulates, and hopes, but there is a lack of actual experiences of the two journeys. For praying and struggling to become once more the breath of a whole culture is, for the present, possible only in small groups. I think of this incomplete book as a contribution toward the realization of this new cultural and political identity.

What will that identity be like? That, too, can only be described in a story-telling, narrative way. The transfiguration of Jesus[3] is both a religious and a religion-critical story which deals with the inward journey and relates it to the return journey. Jesus goes up into the mountain with his three closest friends. "And he was transfigured before them, and his face shone like the sun, and his garments became white as light."[4] Here an experience of God is depicted by means of one of the most profound symbols of good fortune known to biblical tradition: the symbol of the covered countenance that shines like the sun. Fortune, salvation, and blessing are repeatedly portrayed under this imagery. "The Lord make his face to shine upon you,"[5] i.e., look upon you—these are forms of blessing that are preserved in Christian worship services in order to express the experience of good fortune. Paul gives expression to the last expectation of man in this image: "Now we see in a mirror dimly, but then face to face."[6] The face that once was hidden is the farthest point of the inward journey from ego to self in which the light of God is indistinguishable from human light and is entirely "for us." In other words, that means "transfiguration." Jesus passes over from temporal, earthly time into eternal time. Moses and Elijah appear and speak with him on the Mount of Transfiguration.

But again the emphasis of the story is not upon tarrying, nor is there a holding on to religious experience. Peter, who suggests building three tabernacles—one for Jesus, one for Moses, and one for Elijah—is rebuked for his suggestion.[7] What leads Peter to make this suggestion is the temptation inherent in all religion to perpetuate the inward journey and to immerse oneself forever in an act of worship, to hold on to the blessed moment and at the same time to make it a private and priestly moment.

The New Testament story of the Transfiguration is critical of this tendency. In a workers' quarter in Mexico a group of priests and intellectuals are trying to develop a political action. The people there live at the barest imaginable level of existence. There is one telephone for 80,000 people. In the spring of 1975 the group sponsored a political festival to protest a mass raising of rents that had been proposed. They wanted to collect money to engage an attorney who, by negotiation and bribery, would bring the landlords to terms. The festival lasted from 8 A.M. to 8 P.M. and was attended by groups ranging in number from as few as fifty to as many as one thousand. Several bands played and television cameras filmed the proceedings The police observed what went on and kept the participants under control. Those Europeans who were present kept out of sight because their presence was a kind of publicity that might jeopardize the movement.

The festival consisted of a worship service, a demonstration, an open-air play, films produced by the movement, learning games, and teach-ins. The worship service can be described best as a traditional mass with some very untraditional content. The goal is not an enlightened theology but a political theology that is based on the religion of the people. The boycott against rent increases has something to do with Jesus, just as the Christology courses offered have to do with politics. Tradition should not be destroyed but used; people should not be driven out of their religious heritage but made secure in it as something that is an increasingly political reality. The middle- and upper-class group members—including, for example, a doctor who works among the poor for about $150 a month— seek to learn from the people. "We can do nothing without the people," they say, and the practical suggestion of hiring a taxi at a low cost in order to save time is dismissed with the remark, "The people do not ride in taxis."

It is against this background that we must see the worship service that was a major feature of the festival. In that service the story of the Transfiguration was laid hold of and used critically. The three disciples were portrayed as the well-known three monkeys, one of whom covers his ears, another his eyes, and a third his mouth. They hear nothing, see nothing, say nothing! That was a dramatization of the wrong kind of inward journey, the kind that makes religion an opiate of the masses. The program of the festival was a proclamation of the return journey.

How long will the disciples of Jesus be like the three monkeys? We middle-class Europeans are in a situation in which we can tell only about the return journey of others. Our own experiences are too feeble and isolated. Thus the question about the three monkeys is put to us. The question is put to us not to the end that we should omit the inward journey as superfluous, but rather that we should experience that journey as part of our liberation. The monkeys begin to see and hear; no longer will they be silent.

Postscript

The request of the publisher that I write a postscript for inclusion in this book caused me no little uneasiness. To me a book is rather like a baby: once the baby is born, what can you add to it? Nonetheless, I feel that I should give an answer to his question, "How would you have written the book if you had been living in the United States? Would that have made a difference?"

Taking the general theological-political situation into consideration, my reply would have to be in the negative, for there is really no difference between such highly industrialized nations as West Germany and the United States. I am writing for people, not nations. In theory I envisage reaching a very broad reading audience with my writing. In fact—and my mail indicates this to be so—I hope my readers will be teachers and students, social workers, clergy and their parishioners, housewives and their growing children. In fact, I am writing for Christians and post-Christians. In terms of politics they are all citizens of the richest countries in the "first world." Given this situation, any writing may function as a lubricant which keeps the old societies running and helps in the ambiguous business of stabilizing the increasingly unhappy middle class.

It may be that my mental image of the kind of readers I hope to reach is superficial because I envisage my readers in the way I was educated to look at things—in a so-called scientific way. That means I just talked about people and about how I as a writer related to them. I made them into objects. I talked knowingly about where they are, without seeing where they were going. So what I really should say is that I am writing for my brothers and sisters in the hope of finding brothers and sisters. It is a part (perhaps my part) of struggling with the dreadful experience that we are so few. I am searching for allies in the struggle against death by bread alone. It is the unity of struggle and hope that compels me to write.

In this perspective I find an important difference between the old world and the once-new world. It is this difference that finally persuaded me to write this postscript. It would be ever so easy to say that there is more hope over here in the "new world." But perhaps the contrary is true. Perhaps there is even more despair and nausea about the system—and a deeper hate as well. Yet there are more and varied responses to this despair. I find among the friends I have come to know during the first year of my stay in America a different way of questioning. In Europe, leftists would ask a newcomer about his political opinions and positions and whether he belongs to any activist groups. Americans ask about one's life-style. This approach strikes me as more honest and self-critical than the ideologically oriented European approach. The question of life-style presupposes another moral responsibility. How far does your own exodus go? How far have you left the Egypt of capitalism, its wealth and its exploitation, its whole set of values? How much energy do you expend, how much meat (the production of which consumes enough wheat to feed the world's hungry) do you eat? How much of your time do you give to false Gods? These are personal but at the same time political questions, which lead us one step further to the reconciliation between the public and the private spheres of life, the societal and the personal, and help us to overcome the alienation between them that is so characteristic of bourgeois culture.

I have met with many small groups of five to ten people living in the slums of large cities. They work with tenants and organize them in the struggle for their rights. These are people who live in houses that always remind me of my home city Cologne at the end of World War II. There is a new form of poverty among these Christian and often anarchist groups. They live just at the poverty line. They have broken off their educations and careers; they have left their parents and rejected any support they might have gotten from them. They are working part-time and use their freedom to engage in social and political activity. Their life-style is in effect a renunciation and denial of "this world" and its values. And although I cannot see the "return journey" to a humanized society for which I am searching in this book, I see more signs of it, more exodus, more hope.

There is also a difference in spirituality, in my view, between the more skeptical Europeans in secularized societies and the American Christians and their post-Christian sons and daughters. What impresses me most deeply is the existence of a radical Christian tradition in the States, a political and spiritual tradition that takes the side of the oppressed and exploited. This tradition just cannot understand a Christian life apart from the search for justice and peace. There is something like "radical religion" in America. There are people, groups, and movements—too small and too weak, I know, but still alive. I found some salt of the earth here, and coming from a country where it has been illegal since 1972 to teach or publish any form of radicalism, if not indeed to *be* a radical, I have to admit that in the hours and days I spent over the past year with American radicals I felt comfortable and at home.

In Europe a Christian leftist must always apologize for being a Christian, or a church member, or a theologian. When socialists I worked with asked about my profession, I used to say, "I'm a theologian, but . . . ." Coming home for me means that I no longer need to add the "but." I don't have to apologize for loving Christ. So what I found during a year at Union Theological Seminary in New York and by traveling around the country is what I missed so much in my own German Protestant tradition, which I perceive to be unthinkably tamed and corrupted. I would like to express my unwavering hope for the American people as long as some of its sons and daughters are as radical as they are.

On the other hand, this positive feeling sharpens my own doubts about this book. Its relative success in Germany (now in its third printing) raises some uncomfortable questions in my mind. The "inward journey" has been and may be used as a model for escapism into a better "second world." This book, too, is in danger of being read as part of the nostalgic mood in which old reactionaries join with former revolutionary students who have made their peace with the system. This book starts with the single person and works through his or her experiences, and it may therefore be misunderstood as a return to individualism. The search for transcendence may be misread in the sense of the famous Hartford Declaration. Although it shares with the Hartford people the quest for transcending, the book does not approach this question from the same direction at all. Even though it deals with fairy tales instead of production figures, I would like to have the book understood as a contribution to liberation theology, which someday may come to be known as socialist theology.

Within the traditions of the "first world," the tasks of liberation theology will be somewhat different from its tasks in its indigenous "third world." The trouble with middle-class people such as myself is that we are living on both sides. We belong to the exploiters simply by virtue of living here, paying taxes, eating the fruits of the labor of "third world" people and exploiting their cheap labor. But at the same time we are dependent employees, oppressed ourselves by the decision-making classes of our societies. This complex and ambivalent situation has the capacity to confuse and paralyze us. We find ourselves falling either into guilt trips or blind activism and are often unable to participate in the struggle with the necessary revolutionary patience.

The question of how we can deal with the Christian tradition then takes on a new quality. The point is not to secularize the Christian tradition once more but to make it productive for our own presence. We have to be aware of our broken and corrupted tradition as well as of countertraditions that may help us to find a counterlanguage in a world of destroyed and corrupted language. Sometimes I get the impression that secularism in a wide sense was able to secularize only the oppressive traditions of Christianity and not the liberating ones. For example, mothers are subjected to permanent guilt feelings imposed upon them by advertisements. The new god of advertisements punishes as mercilessly as the old one. There are no resources in our society that enable us to live with guilt feelings in the way that confession to a priest did. Secularism did not translate the traditional teaching of hope, trust, and faith; these were simply forgotten, and they died. In this situation, which is somewhat different from that in those countries where liberation theology originated, we here have to emphasize other streams of the tradition. The parts on mysticism in this book have the goal of helping us to reestablish human dignity as it is seen in the Christian tradition, and of bringing mysticism and revolution closer together again. More books on the relation between mysticism and revolution will be written, and this one is meant as a preparation for our return journey into the class struggle. We will spell out our role as brothers and sisters of the Christ who works miracles. Why not we? Why not here? Why not now?

Living in the United States has deepened my hope not only for resistance to death by bread alone—I find a lot of this in Europe too—but for alternatives which are livable now. If "alternative" is another word for "return journey" as a personal, group, and perhaps once-collective experience, then the radical American Christian tradition, which stands in irreconcilable contradiction to the given system, may indeed help us to make our exodus out of Egypt.

The Hegelian-Marxist school has taught us to base our earthly hope on the given contradictions, and in this sense I see a lot of hope in this country. I might have said "for" this country, and that would include the world as well. But that might be saying too much.

Notes

CHAPTER 1
Death by Bread Alone

1. Deut. 8:3; Matt. 4:4.
2. Ps. 88:4.
3. Ps. 88:4–9.
4. Luke 15:11–32.
5. This line from a medieval hymn suggests a liturgical prayer often spoken at burials.
6. See Gen. 4:2–16.
7. Bertolt Brecht, *Gesammelte Werke* (Frankfurt am Main: Suhrkamp, 1966), 12:466.
8. Rom. 6:23.
9. 1 Cor. 15:26
10. See John 11:1–44.
11. See Mark 5:21–24; 35–43.
12. Erich Fromm, *The Heart of Man, Its Genius for Good and Evil* (New York: Harper and Row, 1964), p. 44.
13. 1 John 3:14.
14. See Rom. 8:38–39.
15. Luke 15:32.
16. See Deut. 34:7.

CHAPTER 2
The Fear of Religion

1. Quoted in Edward E. Evans-Pritchard, *Theorien über primitive Religionen* (Frankfurt am Main: Suhrkamp, 1968), p. 62.
2. See Matt. 23:27.
3. Knud E. Løgstrup, "Die Verkündigung Jesu in existenztheologischer und religionsphilosophischer Sicht (Åarhus: unpublished manuscript, 1974).
4. Ibid.
5. Ibid.
6. See Luke 15:24.

CHAPTER 3
The Matter of Experience

1. 2 Cor. 12:9.
2. Gen. 32:24–32.
3. The phrase is from Reimar Lenz.
4. Ronald D. Laing, *Phänomenologie der Erfahrung* (Frankfurt am Main: Suhrkamp, 1970).
5. Reimar Lenz, "Das vergessene Ganze," in *Ev. Kommentare*, July, 1974.
6. Laing, *Phänomenologie*, p. 114.

CHAPTER 4
The Golden Bird

1. Heinrich Seuse [Henry Suso], *Deutsche mystische Schriften* (Düsseldorf: Patmos, 1966), p. 236.
2. Th. W. Adorno, *Minima moralia* (Frankfurt am Main: Suhrkamp, 1962).
3. M. Horkheimer, *Die Sehnsucht nach dem ganz Anderen* (Hamburg: Furche, 1971), p. 69.
4. See P. Worsley, *The Trumpet Shall Sound: A Study of "Cargo" Cults in Melanesia* (London, 1957).
5. The quotation is excerpted from a verse of the Advent hymn "Wake, awake, for night is flying" (*"Wachet auf, ruft uns die Stimme"*). The full text of the lines reads:

Nor eye hath seen, nor ear
Hath yet attained to hear
What there [in heaven] is ours;
But we rejoice, and sing to thee
Our hymn of joy eternally.

6. Hildegunde Wöller, *Die getaufte Revolution: Mythus aus dem Underground* (Munich: Chr. Kaiser, 1973), pp. 7ff.

CHAPTER 5
Elijah on Mount Horeb

1. Ronald D. Laing, *Phänomenologie der Erfahrung* (Frankfurt am Main: Suhrkamp, 1970).
2. David Cooper, *Psychiatrie und Antipsychiatrie* (Frankfurt am Main: Suhrkamp, 1971).
3. Laing, *Phänomenologie*, p. 22.
4. See 1 Kings 18:46.
5. See Erich Fromm, *Psychoanalyse und Religion* (Konstanz, 1966).

CHAPTER 6
The Practice of Meditation

1. See J. Lacarriere, *Die Gott-Trunkenheit* (Wiesbaden: 1967).
2. Shaku Soyen, *Sermons of a Buddhist Abbot* (Chicago, 1906), quoted in Rezepkowski, ed., *Buddhismus in geistiger Welt*, published by *Evangelische Zentralstelle für Weltanschauungsfragen, Arbeitstexte* Number 12, 1973. See Heinrich Zimmer, *Philosophie und Religion Indiens* (Frankfurt am Main: Suhrkamp, 1973), p. 353.
3. See "Meditation" in *Alternativen*, Heft 8 (Munich: Kösel, 1971).
4. Zimmer, *Philosophie*, p. 334.
5. W. Oehl, ed., *Deutsche Mystikerbriefe des Mittelalters 1100–1550* (1931); reprint (Darmstadt: Wissenschaftliche Buchgesellschaft, 1972), p. 637.
6. Heinrich Seuse [Henry Suso], *Deutsche mystische Schriften* (Düsseldorf: Patmos, 1966), p. 416.

CHAPTER 7
Deny God for God's Sake

1. Heinrich Seuse [Henry Suso], *Deutsche mystische Schriften* (Düsseldorf: Patmos, 1966), p. 416.
2. *Meister Eckhart, Deutsche Predigten und Traktate*, ed. J. Quint (Munich: Hanser, 1969), p. 185.
3. W. Oehl, ed., *Deutsche Mystikerbriefe des Mittelalters 1100–1550* (1931); reprint (Darmstadt: Wissenschaftliche Buchgesellschaft, 1972), p. 637.
4. Gal. 2:20.
5. Eckhart, *Deutsche Predigten*, p. 308. See also Dorothee Soelle, *Suffering* (Philadelphia: Fortress Press, 1975), pp. 93–99.
6. Eckhart, *Deutsche Predigten*, p. 180. The conclusion of the text warrants the assumption that this was stated in an actual letter, probably one written to a nun.
7. Oehl, *Deutsche Mystikerbriefe*, pp. 634–35.
8. Seuse, *Deutsche mystische Schriften*, pp. 33, 169.
9. Oehl, *Deutsche Mystikerbriefe*, p. 307.
10. Seuse, *Deutsche mystische Schriften*, p. 341.
11. Ibid.
12. The stanza reads in German:

> In deine Lieb' versenken
> Will ich mich ganz und gar,
> Mein Herz will ich dir schenken,
> Und alles was ich hab'.

13. Oehl, *Deutsche Mystikerbriefe*, p. 317.
14. Hildegunde Wöller, *Die getaufte Revolution: Mythus aus dem Underground* (Munich: Chr. Kaiser, 1973), pp. 40–41.
15. See Dorothee Soelle, *Realisation: Studien zum Verhältnis von Theologie und Dichtung nach der Aufklärung* (Neuwied: Luchterhand, 1973), p. 262, concerning Jean Paul.
16. The German text reads:

> O Mutter, halte dein Kindlein warm
> Die Welt ist kalt und helle.

17. Eckhart, *Deutsche Predigten*, p. 180.

18. Ibid.
19. Seuse, *Deutsche mystische Schriften*, p. 416.

CHAPTER 8
A Student's Letter

1. Tobias Brocher, *Von der Schwierigkeit zu lieben* (Stuttgart: Kreuz Verlag, 1975), pp. 9–11.
2. Erik H. Erikson, *Kindheit und Gesellschaft* (Stuttgart: Klett, 1968), p. 256.
3. Erik H. Erikson, *Einsicht und Verantwortung* (Stuttgart: Klett, 1966), p. 186.
4. See Dorothee Soelle, *Das Recht ein anderer zu werden* (Neuwied: Luchterhand, 1971), pp. 61ff.
5. See Luke 15:3–7.
6. Leland Elhard, "Living Faith: Some Contributions of the Concept of the Ego-Identity to the Understanding of Faith," in *The Dialogue Between Theology and Psychology* (1968), pp. 39, 153.
7. See Mark 2:9.
8. David Cooper, *Psychiatrie und Antipsychiatrie* (Frankfurt am Main: Suhrkamp, 1971), p. 95.
9. Mark 10:17–22.

CHAPTER 9
But When the Bright and Morning Star Arises

1. Heinrich Seuse [Henry Suso], *Deutsche mystische Schriften* (Düsseldorf: Patmos, 1966), p. 241.
2. Ibid., pp. 401ff.
3. Erik H. Erikson, *Kindheit und Gesellschaft* (Stuttgart: Klett, 1968), p. 244.
4. See Rev. 2:28 and 22:16.
5. Meister Eckhart, *Deutsche Predigten und Traktate*, ed. J. Quint (Munich: Hanser, 1969), p. 199.

CHAPTER 10
Who Am I?

1. In Dietrich Bonhoeffer, *Widerstand und Ergebung* (Munich: Chr. Kaiser, 1954), pp. 242–43; 1970 ed., pp. 381–82.

2. Erik H. Erikson, *Einsicht und Verantwortung* (Stuttgart: Klett, 1966), p. 135.

3. Erich Fromm, *Das Christusdogma und andere Essays* (Munich, 1975), p. 175.

4. Ibid.

5. Ibid., p. 176.

CHAPTER 11
Psalm 139

1. 1 John 3:2.

CHAPTER 12
The Wish to Be Whole

1. Acts 1:9–11.

2. Acts 1:11.

3. Mark 9:2–8.

4. Matt. 17:2.

5. Num. 6:24–26.

6. 1 Cor. 13:12.

7. Mark 9:5.

CPSIA information can be obtained
at www.ICGtesting.com
Printed in the USA
LVHW051616290321
682837LV00011B/1539

9 781592 441921